MW01087610

Praise for *White Fear*

"Roland Martin is one of the great journalists of our time! And his love of Black people is legendary! This book is another grand example of his brilliance and courage!"

—Dr. Cornel West

"America is spinning out of control. But as most pundits struggle to understand why, Roland Martin nails it: what rests at the heart of the nation's chaos is White Fear of multiracial, pluralistic democracy. For 400 years that fear has been cultivated by elites to divide and conquer working people with common interests. And now the country's very future is at risk. Thankfully, Martin shows us a way out of the mess, if the nation is prepared to listen."

—Tim Wise, author of *White Like Me* and
Dispatches from the Race War

"The proliferation of groups of 'White' people protesting the progress of those who are classified as other than 'White', is the result of the fear among 'White' people that they are going to lose their numerical majority in the USA. That we 'White' people have always been in the numerical minority all over the globe has been carefully ignored, or denied, for over 250 years. It's time to tell the truth about who our earliest citizens were, and, by so doing, give those who are descendants of those earliest citizens the information about the brilliance of those who came before us, and who will be here long after we 'White' folks have gone. Once we get this information into every classroom in the US, we will all stop seeing 'race' as real and start appreciating all of us as we are."

—Jane Elliott, anti-racist lecturer, author, and creator of
the world-renowned "Blue Eyes/Brown Eyes Exercise"

"Fear is at the root of almost every injustice—fear of the other, fear that is created by false assumptions, or fear created by a desire for power. Roland Martin's book addresses a particular kind of fear that has been both the backdrop and forefront of racism in this country. White Fear has been used and created by extremist forces to turn people who need each other against one another while the forces promoting the fear loot and take from people on both sides. This is an important read for all people, regardless of your race and color. Understand White Fear so you can release and resist it."

—Rev. Dr. William J. Barber II, author of
We Are Called to Be a Movement

"How can you NOT read a book with THIS title?! Roland always tells it like it is. This book is no different— GOSPEL truth. The question here for White folks is timely, and is incumbent upon them to answer: what will you do with your fear and how will you respond to this clarion call?"

—Angela Rye, CEO of IMPACT Strategies
and former CNN commentator

"Roland Martin has always been such a necessary voice to the national discourse. He beautifully occupies space at the intersection of journalism, Blackness, and truth telling, and he does so brilliantly in his new book *White Fear*. His latest book is not only a warning call to America but also an example of why Black media ownership is integral in the telling of our stories, and offers our perspectives in ways that are unfiltered, unapologetic, and unfettered. This literary wakeup call is a must-read."

—Tiffany Cross, host of MSNBC's *The Cross Connection*

"Roland Martin has always candidly and courageously served as the eyes and ears for Black America while giving us a voice and inspiring us with a vision of what should and could be. In his new book, *White Fear*, he has put a literary mirror to America, in general, and White folks in particular. Mirrors are designed for us to see things as they really are so we can correct what is wrong. This 'mirror' will help White America find its mind so that all of us can create a nation that becomes true to what it has always claimed it wants to be. The future of this nation depends on how it responds to this 'mirror!'"

—Rev. Dr. Frederick D. Haynes III, senior pastor,
Friendship-West Baptist Church, Dallas, Texas

WHITE FEAR

Also by Roland S. Martin

Listening to the Spirit Within
50 Perspectives on Faith

Speak, Brother!
A Black Man's View of America

The First
President Barak Obama's Road to the White House
as Originally Reported by Roland S. Martin

WHITE FEAR

HOW THE BROWNING OF AMERICA IS MAKING WHITE FOLKS LOSE THEIR MINDS

ROLAND S. MARTIN

WITH LEAH LAKINS

BenBella Books, Inc.
Dallas, TX

White Fear copyright © 2022 by Nu Vision Media, Inc.

All rights reserved. Except in the case of brief quotations embodied in critical articles or reviews, no part of this book may be used or reproduced, stored, transmitted, or used in any manner whatsoever, including for training artificial intelligence (AI) technologies or for automated text and data mining, without prior written permission from the publisher.

BenBella Books, Inc.
8080 N. Central Expressway
Suite 1700
Dallas, TX 75206
benbellabooks.com
Send feedback to feedback@benbellabooks.com

BenBella is a federally registered trademark.

Printed in the United States of America
10 9 8 7

Library of Congress Control Number: 2022013466
ISBN 9781637740286 (hardcover)
ISBN 9781637740293 (ebook)

Editing by Leah Wilson and Joe Rhatigan
Copyediting by Elizabeth Degenhard
Proofreading by Greg Teague and Cape Cod Compositors, Inc.
Text design and composition by PerfecType, Nashville, TN
Cover design by Brian Lemus
Cover photo of the Jan. 6, 2021, U.S. Capitol Riot © Getty Images News /
   Brent Stirton
Printed by Lake Book Manufacturing

Special discounts for bulk sales are available. Please contact bulkorders@benbellabooks.com.

CONTENTS

INTRODUCTION

By 2043, no ethnic group will be the majority in America.

Two thirds of the world's countries are already composed of a majority of people of color and—sooner than we know it—America will be just like the rest of the world.

In fact, a 2018 Pew Research Study showed that almost half (49 percent) of post-millennials (ages six to twenty-one) are Hispanic, African American, and Asian. By 2043, these growth trends among people of color will continue, and it is expected that less than 47 percent of the country will be White Americans. The political impact of these numbers can already be seen in the high turnout of millennials and post-millennials in the 2018 midterm elections. According to Axios, an estimated 31 percent of eighteen- to twenty-nine-year-olds voted, which was the highest voter turnout for that age group since 1994. These rapidly changing demographics will have a profound impact in the next two decades for our elections, government policies, economic growth, and a whole lot more.

Does this scare you?

The answer to that question might just depend on the color of your skin.

———————

White supremacy has been at the foundation of this country's infrastructure since the first enslaved Africans arrived on the shores of Jamestown, Virginia, in 1619, and it continues to have a lasting impact in this country. Racial division has defined America, and race continues to dominate the American psyche like no other. In fact, race is so embedded in the DNA of America that most of us are unaware of how deeply it affects how we live, move, and breathe.

While the Thirteenth, Fourteenth, and Fifteenth Amendments, the Civil Rights Acts of 1866 and 1964, the Voting Rights Act of 1965, and the Fair Housing Act of 1968 provided necessary legislation and policy to give African Americans basic civil rights, these policies did not address the underlying, fundamental problem of why we needed to create legislation to address these issues in the first place: *White Fear*.

Why is it so important to understand White Fear? Without a proper understanding of this pulsating insanity and the history behind it, we will continue to be blindsided every time White Fear inevitably rears its head.

I define White Fear as the unwillingness to share power and resources and allow for the redefinition of America's morals, values, and principles. White Fear is perpetuated by White Americans who are resistant to allowing America to live up to the promises of the Constitution and the Declaration of Independence.

When I interviewed anti-racism educator Jane Elliott on my show *Roland Martin Unfiltered* in 2019, she summed up White Fear brilliantly: "The problem with white people is not white innocence. Nor is it white privilege. The problem is white ignorance. And until we get educated to the fact that we are not superior just because we have a lack of melanin in our skin, that's how long we will have this problem. No one is responsible for the past. We are all responsible for the present and the future that we're creating for ourselves and our children."

Recognizing White Fear isn't just about pointing out overt symbols of hooded Klan members and burning crosses. It's about calling out voter suppression laws, gerrymandering, redlining, predatory loans, underfunded school systems, gentrification, police brutality, and any other practices that prevent people of color from taking equal part in the American Dream.

———

Without appropriately addressing White Fear, we aren't doing anything more than spraying air freshener in a room filled with dog shit. When we don't address White Fear, American classrooms will continue to be even more segregated than they were before *Brown v. Board of Education*. When we ignore White Fear, people of color will continue to be redlined into poorer, under-served neighborhoods and gentrified out of communities where they have lived and built family legacies for generations. When we are lulled into the false notion that White Fear has been erased by the election of the nation's first African American president, he is replaced by a White supremacist who has done more to enforce the racial divide than any American leader in more than thirty years.

This book is a call for White Americans to take a hard look in the mirror and begin dealing with their own internal racial conflicts. It is designed to be a conversation piece for White Americans to start the necessary reprogramming of their thoughts, assumptions, and beliefs about this country, especially as it relates to race. It also sounds the alarm for White Americans to understand that the demographics and cultural norms of America are changing—regardless of whether they are ready or not. Therefore, White Americans either need to face their bigotry and shift into the reality of a swiftly changing America or be locked out of the reality of the New American Dream.

White Fear is also a call to action for people of color to begin recognizing and stepping into new opportunities in entrepreneurship, corporate development, local and national leadership, and economic empowerment as the dynamics of power begin to shift in this country. Recognizing the debilitating, demoralizing, and damaging effects of White supremacy is just the first step.

White Fear will be a necessary tool for people of color to begin building their resources, developing their skills sets, and appropriately strategizing their moves to dismantle White supremacy and usher in the America that they deserve.

This book also presents my unapologetic take on what is happening today. From Black Lives Matter to challenging corporate media on their racial blind spots to fighting voter suppression, I have never shied away from speaking truth to power and telling it like it is. I make it perfectly clear throughout this book that this racial divide will not end with Donald Trump. We are in the midst of a racial war that will define what kind of nation we have for the next generation.

White Fear is about connecting the puzzle pieces about the pervasive nature of White Fear and educating people about the inevitable escalation of violence and tension that will continue as the demographics of this country swiftly change from majority White to a majority of Black, Latino, and Asian Americans. We have to begin preparing the next generation for this change. The prevalence of White Fear will cause the political and economic landscape of America to get a whole lot worse before it gets any better.

Finally, *White Fear* will identify these separate puzzle pieces, from Trump's rise to the U.S. presidency to the decline of White American optimism to the diminishing blue-collar workforce, and create the larger picture of what will unfold in America over the next two decades. White Fear is a significant issue in our country, and we have to prepare ourselves for it. This is why *White Fear* matters—and why it matters *right now*.

IGNITING THE FLAME OF WHITE FEAR

White Fear is always a fire waiting to start. Let's take a look at a few of the things that ignite the fire of White Fear, including politicians (past and present), the media, and other talking heads, gerrymandering, coded rhetoric, and even the minimizing of an insurrection.

CHAPTER ONE

THE KINDLING FOR WHITE FEAR

While working as a contributor for CNN right after Barack Obama's first election, I had a conversation with my colleague John Avlon, author of the 2010 book *Wingnuts: How the Lunatic Fringe Is Hijacking America*. We were discussing the premise of his book, and I said, "John, we're living in the beginning of White minority resistance."

John said, "How so?"

I then shared with him a recent poll that was released near the inauguration of the nation's first Black president, Barack Hussein Obama. The basic question was whether Americans were optimistic about the future of America.

What stood out to me was that a majority of every ethnic group—Blacks, Latinos, and Asians—said they were optimistic about the future. Yet White Americans were the only group that fell below a majority. That simple question raised a host of issues for me, and despite all of the proclamations of a so-called "post-racial America" (which I knew was utter bullshit), I knew that there would be a fierce response from White America to the emergence of this Black man in the White House.

In fact, within hours of Obama's last inaugural ball, then Senate minority leader Mitch McConnell made it clear that his primary goal was to make Barack Obama a one-term president. Many may say that was just a typical Republican response to a Democrat in office, but it cut even deeper as soon as he began to lead.

In Obama's first term, the Tea Party came to prominence. While its adherents would say they were merely individuals who were upset with billionaires and Wall Street being bailed out, their anger and righteous indignation serve as a supple home to extremist voices. Some folks claimed that Obama would introduce White slavery; they spewed xenophobic and racist remarks; and they continued circulating the idea of birtherism (otherwise known as the total falsehood that Obama was not born in the United States).

The election of President Obama woke up White America to the reality that the country was headed in a new direction . . . and this change was not going to go down easy.

But, of course, Mitch McConnell's agenda and the rise of the Tea Party were nothing new. In fact, America has a long history of aggrieved White people being angry with any initiatives that helped Black people.

Abraham Lincoln had not even been elected president when forces in the South began to suggest that if he was elected and dared to free the slaves, there would be Civil War in America. And that is exactly what happened. It wasn't a battle over states' rights or some other silly rationale provided by lovers of the Confederacy. It was about freedom for Black people.

Once the war ended, radical Republicans continued their march for Black freedom, passing the Thirteenth, Fourteenth, and Fifteenth Amendments, what became known as the Reconstruction Amendments. These were not passed in a bipartisan manner. While Democrats tried to stop them, the Republicans moved full force ahead.

Yet as the Reconstruction period progressed, White Americans began to get tired of the legislative efforts to help freed slaves. Not even a week after the Civil War ended, Lincoln was assassinated and southerner Andrew Johnson became president, making his racist views clear, which served as fuel for the forces that desired to keep Blacks from succeeding. Tensions ramped up considerably with the contested election of 1876 and the eventual Compromise of 1877, in which southerners agreed to Rutherford B. Hayes becoming president as long as federal troops were removed from the last three remaining southern state capitols. That federal occupation had provided protection to freed slaves, who saw rapid advancement and election to office. Once the Compromise was agreed to, southern Democrats picked up their reign of terror, leading to eighty-eight years of Jim Crow.

Not only did the resistance to Black advancement pick up considerably in southern states, even the White supremacist Supreme Court played a role, declaring the Civil Rights Act of 1875 unconstitutional, determining that Congress did not have the power to outlaw discrimination. There would not be another civil rights act in America until 1957.

Then in 1890, the war on Black advancement continued in Mississippi, where White supremacists held a constitutional convention to stop the political advancement of Blacks. In the days after Reconstruction, Blacks were elected all across the South and especially in Mississippi. After years of Black leaders coming into legislative power throughout the state, members of the Mississippi state legislature cried out, "There are too many Blacks being elected! We have to end this now!" They changed their state constitution to limit Black voting rights and made it harder for Black candidates to run for office. Since 1890, not a single African American has been elected to statewide office in Mississippi.

And White Fear didn't stop in Mississippi. It traveled up the coast to Wilmington, North Carolina, in 1898, when a group of White supremacists staged an insurrection to overthrow a group of rightfully elected White and Black leaders who sought to bring equality to the city.

We saw it again with the destruction and massacre in Tulsa, Oklahoma, in 1921.

And again at the doors of Central High School in Little Rock, Arkansas, in 1957.

And again with the assassination of Martin Luther King Jr. on April 4, 1968.

And again with the violent implosions from mandatory busing and school integration in the 1970s.

And again with the Crime Bill passed by President Bill Clinton in 1994.

And again with the *Shelby County v. Holder* verdict in 2013, which gutted major provisions to the Voting Rights Act of 1965.

And again with the election of Donald J. Trump on November 9, 2016.

And again with the Capitol insurrection on January 6, 2021.

And again . . .

and again . . .

and again.

What we have seen in American history is that Black success is always followed by White backlash. Whether triggered by the fear of Blacks in positions of power or the fear that Black folks would take White Americans' jobs, this backlash has been the consistent pattern in this country.

These mere highlights of ignited White Fear from history are just the tip of the iceberg of what happens when White American power is threatened by Black people and other people of color asserting their rights to have access to what they deserve.

January 6, 2021, marked almost twelve years to the day that I made that declaration to John Avlon about the oncoming onslaught of White minority resistance. When people asked me, "Roland, what was your reaction to what took place on January sixth?" I said, "I smiled."

Why? Because America finally got to see what we as African Americans have always seen and predicted: White folks lose their minds due to Black success. Oh, you think I'm wrong? What were the four American cities Donald Trump kept citing as his proof of a rigged election? Atlanta, Philadelphia, Detroit, and Milwaukee. What are those often called? *Black cities*. He paid for a partial recount of votes in Wisconsin—in Milwaukee. America could not escape the reality of White Fear led by a racist president who fueled racist rhetoric that propelled other White Americans to attempt to overthrow the U.S. government. While mainstream media ignored this oncoming insurrection for years, anyone with a functional grasp of American history could have accurately predicted that as soon as White power is threatened, the violent effects of White Fear are never far behind.

CHAPTER TWO

ENTER DONALD TRUMP

Let me repeat: By 2043, no ethnic group will be the majority in America.

Fear of this fact had already begun to grip the nation by the mid-2010s. Many White Americans felt that America was losing its way. We had become a nation overrun with illegal immigrants. A nation where wokeism, political correctness, and equality had rendered us impotent to the America we used to be. Our standing in the world was being destroyed because we were not the country of yesteryear—if only we could return to being a shining city on a hill, a time when things were so simple. Oh, and when Black folks were being violently oppressed and lynched. Just go back and look at the political messaging of Ronald Reagan in 1980; Bob Dole in 1996; and even the racist and incendiary politics of Pat Buchanan. The White Fear of Buchanan was once seen as the fringe nut cases, a group of folks who were always pissed off and wanted to see someone do something.

Enter Donald Trump—and a new era of unapologetic White nationalism.

From day one, Trump's presidential campaign was the energy boost that White America wanted and needed. When he descended the escalator at Trump Tower on June 16, 2015, to announce his bid for the presidency, he went straight to the heart of the trifecta of White American angst: illegal immigrants, law and order, and political correctness.

In a May 2018 *New York Times* article, Diana C. Mutz of the University of Pennsylvania further argued that "White voters fell for Mr. Trump because they felt threatened by increasing numbers of minorities and the sense that the United States was losing its global dominance."

Trump put an unapologetic voice to White Fear. He brazenly voiced what many wanted to utter out loud but were too afraid to say. He said it and didn't give a damn what others thought. And mainstream media, always wanting the ratings, *loved it*. We saw him foam at the mouth during his rallies to nearly all White crowds. They cheered him on when he slammed Black Lives Matter. He became their Great White Hope. He was their White savior after America's first Black president, Barack Hussein Obama.

"Make America Great Again!"

"Take back our country!"

"The good old days are here again!"

In 2009, a poll from the Pew Research Center caught my attention and led me to the conclusion that race relations were about to become even more real. This is the same poll I later discussed with my colleague John Avlon. It asked the following question: "Are you optimistic about the future of America for your children?"

It was a fairly easy question, yet the results were striking. A majority of every ethnic group said they were optimistic about the future, except for one: White Americans. Only 41 percent of White Americans said they were optimistic about the future of America for their children. Why?

White Americans instinctively knew that their White privilege was coming to an end. Their children would now have to compete in environments where White people never had to compete before. White folks dominated everything in America. Now their good thing was coming to an end.

And this is how we ignite White Fear.

Even though White Americans are still the dominant majority, when you see the minority population as a collective, their sheer numbers threaten that superiority. Conservative talking heads such as Bill O'Reilly, Glenn Beck, Sean Hannity, Laura

Ingraham, and Tucker Carlson began to use their platforms to expound on White grievance and act as if White Americans were in the minority. Then, fast-forward to the election of Donald Trump and guess what we find? These pessimistic ideas about the future of our country had gotten worse.

In September 2016, the Pew Research Center asked Americans if they were optimistic about the economy during the next ten years. The group with the lowest wealth—African Americans—had the highest optimism. Latino Americans had the second-lowest wealth and the second-highest optimism, followed by Asian Americans. Meanwhile, White Americans had the lowest economic optimism even though they had the highest wealth. How can the group who has the most wealth have the lowest optimism? Because they couldn't partake in all the spoils. They had no choice but to share, and they were scared their children would get beat out of opportunities they viewed as their birthright. Even though White Americans received the most government assistance of any ethnic group in this country, most still decried welfare and handouts.

White privilege doesn't mean that if you're White, you automatically live in a gated community, drive a Rolls-Royce, and play croquet or polo. The truth is that many White Americans are high school graduates living on minimum wage and residing in rural America. The privilege is not demonstrated in how much money they have in their retirement account but in the fact that they can go to their local Walmart without having someone think that they are capable of stealing merchandise off the shelf.

The power of White supremacy is that it doesn't matter if you're White with money. Whiteness, itself, is a currency. The power of Whiteness means that you get to define and decide what the worldview will be. When you look at the viral video of the female Trump supporter who was sprayed with mace during the Capitol insurrection in January 2021, she passionately said, "We're storming the Capitol, it's a revolution!" She was defending her right to protest in defense of Trump's baseless claims that he won the 2020 election, and she assumed her Whiteness made it okay to commit a crime. Why is this important for us to understand? Threatening the agenda and the power dynamics invokes an endless cycle of White Fear. White values set the agenda and determine who has power. Even when White voters are clearly voting against their own economic, health, and civil interests, they are actually voting for Whiteness. This currency of Whiteness is powerful because of the long-term, systemic effects that it continues to have on this nation.

MORE FUEL FOR THE FIRE

January 6, 2021, put a definitive stake in the ground. America's reckoning with Whiteness will be defined before this date and after this date. This is no longer about Donald Trump. The bloodshed of this moment is on the Republican Party. Republicans, and the nation, cannot move forward without taking a stand.

When you have insurrections, you are *supposed to take down insurrectionists!* We already saw how Donald Trump's supporters stormed the capitols of Michigan, Idaho, and Wisconsin in the spring of 2020. Therefore, it is unfathomable that there was still a debate about how to deal with insurrectionists weeks after this blatant attack on the U.S. Capitol. We have to be honest about the insanity of that moment and the fact that Donald Trump gave them the green light. There has to be a reckoning within the Republican Party. There is no way to explain away the events of January 6.

We have to get this picture in our mind: The Secret Service detail for the vice president, the vice president-elect, and the speaker of the House were all in an active 360-degree armed defense to protect their constituents on the House and Senate floors. We haven't seen that kind of active armed engagements to protect members of Congress or the White House since Ronald Reagan was shot in 1980. We have to call this what it was—a national security emergency.

However, White violence is often excused and minimized. White violence is somehow justified, with the media immediately putting forth this angelic image of a person who is just struggling with mental illness. Or battling economic anxiety, even though an analysis of those attending that day were not poor, uneducated Whites. They were middle- and upper-income Whites. The reality is that the vast number of domestic terrorist incidents in this country are committed by White men who are aligned with White supremacist ideology.

We also have to recognize that Donald Trump allowed this insurrection to take place. If this was not a Donald Trump show, the FBI would have been deployed within five minutes. If this was a group that wasn't all White, there would have been FBI agents and National Guard members running down Pennsylvania Avenue to protect the president and the Capitol. Donald Trump radicalized millions of people in this country, and if you think that kind of damage and rage left the White House on January 20, you've got another thing coming.

The buildup to this insurrection wasn't helped by the media filling every twenty-four-hour cycle with daunting statistics about job losses from traditional American industrial industries, minority political candidates opposing long-term White incumbents, and immigrants threatening to flood American borders and take away American resources. When I began writing this book in 2018, Donald Trump's campaign and ascent to the presidency was a clear reaction to eight years of Barack Obama. For eight years, all White America heard, especially from conservative news commentators, was that America was weak. They repeatedly touted that America was bending its will to every other country. These talking heads found every way imaginable to declare that President Obama was weak and that he alone was destroying what made America great.

That kind of stark language was music to the ears of many aggrieved White Americans who felt as if their America was going by the wayside. Listen to the rhetoric that was being spewed on conservative talk radio and by prominent conservative cable pundits such as Tucker Carlson, Laura Ingraham, Bill O'Reilly, and Sean Hannity. All you heard was a constant loop of fear mongering that repeated the refrain, "We're losing the American way and what made us great."

When you begin to understand the kind of language that tickles the ears of White America, you can see why Donald Trump was able to assemble a coalition of rabid followers to his rallies in droves. And when you also appeal to the Chamber of Commerce Republicans, the National Defense Republicans, and the Evangelicals, you now have the makings of the Trump presidency.

White Fear has also been slowly stoked for the last thirty years by census and population experts who have been predicting that America would soon become a majority-minority nation. White America would no longer have their precious majority that they've been tightly holding onto since the founding of this nation.

Many people were skeptical when they first heard these predictions. Some folks declared, "I'll be long dead before that happens." But the following three things happened:

- White Americans stopped having as many babies.
- Black Americans kept having children.
- Latino Americans did not stop having children.

As a result, the White population was not able to keep up with the changing demographics. In 2016, the majority of children in the nation's public schools were Black and Brown. The White population was also decimated by the opioid crisis. The death rate for White Americans from this epidemic skyrocketed in Connecticut, New Hampshire, Vermont, and West Virginia. In November 2016, *Time* magazine reported that the White death rate would surpass the White birth rate in seventeen states.

CHAPTER THREE

FOLLOWING RONALD REAGAN'S PLAYBOOK

et me return now for a moment to the Republican Party. We have to look at the turmoil that's been allowed to fester within the party for the last decade. From the vicious rollbacks on *Roe v. Wade* and women's rights to gerrymandering in districts throughout the country to the nonstop assault on Obamacare, you have to stop and wonder if the Republican Party even gives a damn about the American people.

When we focus on gerrymandering in particular, you can look back at the blatant racist policies of the king of gerrymandering and Republican political strategist, the late Thomas Hofeller, and see that the seeds of the current Republican party were starting to blow as early as the 2010 midterm elections. Hofeller was heralded as a pioneer of modern redistricting as he helped states such as North Carolina and Georgia severely dilute the Black vote.

Fast-forward to 2018, and we can see the vicious underhanded attacks on Black Democratic candidates Stacey Abrams in Georgia and Andrew Gillum in Florida. Their respective Republican challengers did everything in their power to defame their characters while also enforcing ridiculous voting ID laws. Instead of hiding behind all this foolish voter suppression, why doesn't the Republican Party just come out and say, "We don't want y'all to show up at the polls and take away our power!"

Now, when we get back to the nightmare that was the Trump presidency, we can see clear as day that not only is there a Blacklash, but there's also a backlash on Latinos, Muslims, immigrants, and transgender people—essentially anyone who is not White or anyone who is a threat to Donald Trump's fragile ego.

But the story of Donald Trump and the American nightmare we're now living in is no different from what we heard from White Americans in 1976 and 1980 when Ronald Reagan ran for president. Reagan opened his campaign by advocating for states' rights. His language wasn't as overt as George Wallace or Barry Goldwater, but he used his charm as a former actor to say the very things that White Americans wanted to hear. The exit polling data from the 1980 general election showed that 25 to 30 percent of people who voted felt that the Democrats were doing too much for Black people.

Throughout his campaign, Reagan spoke right to the heart of White Fear within these aggrieved people. Reagan's campaign was the first to speak to White America's frustration about Black people by using dog whistle language such as "Welfare Queens," "Jungle Paths," and "Restoring Law and Order." During his 1976 campaign, he told the story of a Black mother in Chicago, Linda Taylor, who allegedly used fifty Social Security numbers to secure $150,000 in social benefits. Although this story was soundly refuted several times, and even though more Whites than Blacks benefit from welfare services, the image of the Black Welfare Queen would persist throughout American politics for years.

Ronald and Nancy Reagan further represented the picture-perfect ideal of Ozzie and Harriet-type family structure with a husband, wife, two children, and a picket fence. The Reagans contrasted this idealistic picture against the reality of a quickly shifting America with the Civil Rights Movement, the Women's Liberation Movement, and the resistance to the war in Vietnam. When his campaign contrasted these two Americas, it was fertile ground to make White America hearken back to a seemingly easier and simpler time. Thus was born the campaign slogan that would launch him into a landslide victory into the American presidency: "Let's Make America Great Again." Sound familiar?

As governor of California, Ronald Reagan regularly talked about providing fair housing and removing the "Jungle Paths" of Black communities to good neighborhoods. He defended the idea that Whites did not have to sell their homes to Black families. This ideology was further perpetuated by Nancy Reagan's refusal to live in the state capitol in Sacramento because of its close proximity to everyday Californians.

Housing discrimination isn't just about lower property values or not being able to impress your neighbors; the physical location of your home has an effect on how you work and live. Local property taxes are what fund local school districts, which then impacts school quality; they're also what pays for street cleaning, recycling, and other community benefits.

The reality is that residential segregation in every metropolitan area was created by our government via explicit racial policies, and this history was once well known . . . but we've forgotten it. Unless we relearn this history, we're not going to be able to remedy it. If we understand that government created racial segregation, then we understand that it's unconstitutional. Racial segregation by neighborhood is just as unconstitutional as segregating water fountains or buses or restaurants or any of the other institutions that used to be segregated. Black folks were shut out of owning and being able to resell a home, which contributes to gaps in schooling, wealth, and income in this country.

The reason why it is so important to understand Ronald Reagan as a predecessor to Donald Trump is because White Fear before Reagan had been primarily defined as Southern leaders resisting integration and voting rights in Southern states. But here we have a West

Coast politician who spoke out against the racial uprising in Watts in 1965 and developed legislation to ban the Black Panthers from their Second Amendment rights to own guns in 1968. The White Fear that he stoked in California shows up for his gubernatorial success in the 1960s when he stood with White voters regarding racially discriminatory housing and later in his first run for president in 1976 and again in his eventual victory over Jimmy Carter in 1980. When he becomes president, we are ushered into twelve years of White Fear in the White House from his re-election in 1984 to the victory of his vice president, George H. W. Bush, in 1988. Reagan was able to ride this train of White Fear into political victory because he understood that Whiteness, itself, has a currency.

When Donald Trump announced his bid for the presidency on June 16, 2015, many people considered his presidential run to be a joke. For a number of months, he polled at around 1 percent. When you look at what Donald Trump did in that opening speech on the escalator—the attack on immigrants, the strongman talk about how America needs to be more powerful and have a strong leader—he was doing exactly what Reagan and others have done before him. He was stoking White America's deepest fears. When Donald Trump showed up, he became the living embodiment of those eight years of White Fear during Obama's presidency.

Donald Trump tapped right into this fear and picked up on the same language to continue promoting these racist ideals throughout his campaign. There were many political experts and talking heads who believed that Donald Trump became more of an embodiment of ultra-conservative commentator Pat Buchanan's ideals about America than Buchanan himself. Trump's appeal to White America was that he said exactly what he felt and didn't care about falling in line with the optics of the GOP. He articulated what many of these established GOP members always wanted to say. To be clear, Donald Trump simply made public what was always there. He found the right time in America, after two terms of America's first Black president, to ignite White Fear and unleash a fury of racism that we hadn't seen in a generation.

I knew everything was off the table when Donald Trump attacked John McCain as a prisoner of war and the GOP went along with it, saying, "We're fine with that." There is nothing more powerful and emotional to America, especially White America, than a POW. POWs are American heroes. When there is no penalty for attacking one of America's most beloved war heroes, nothing is sacred.

White America was so hungry for the vitriol that Trump was serving that the first two GOP presidential candidates to drop out in 2016 were Tim Pawlenty, the former governor of Minnesota, and Scott Walker, the then-governor of Wisconsin. Conventional political strategy would clearly put these two midwestern Republican governors at the forefront of this race. Both governors had wide appeal to rural voters and spoke authoritatively to

White America. But when you've had eight years of Black power threatening to continue to upset the status quo of White America, Perry and Walker never stood a chance to become viable candidates.

One by one, Trump took down sixteen established GOP politicians until he won the nomination. The key to Trump's nomination wasn't winning over 100 percent of the Republican Party. All he needed was 30 percent of the voting block during the primary season to keep winning. Winning builds momentum. He continued to win throughout the primaries, and White voters began coalescing around him. At that point, the GOP was afraid to truly take him on in a hardcore way. They did not want to go after him and upset his base. Trump did a good job of carrying his supporters and plugging into White Fear.

By the time of the Republican convention, it was too late to stop him. The Republican nomination was based on the winner taking it all, and with just 30 percent of the vote, Trump handily won all the delegates. Next thing you knew, he controlled the party.

So in truth, Donald Trump did the exact same thing that Ronald Reagan, the John Birch Society, and the Tea Party did before him— he appealed to aggrieved White Americans who felt like they were losing their country. He evoked the same racist rhetorical tools as Richard Nixon in his campaigns. All the rhetoric and fear built up to a point where he was able to tap into that White resentment and ride that White Fear all the way to the White House.

What Donald Trump and the Republican Party want to create is an alternate universe that extends beyond Fox News and into society to perpetuate how we learn about American history. The goal is to have an authoritarian government, run by a White man, held down by White men. It doesn't matter who gets bulldozed over; it will be mostly Black and Brown people, but there will be White casualties as well. It should be evident by now that this is all about one domineering group maintaining power, equal rights be damned. We must challenge the White newsrooms to stop being comfortable and to start calling things what they are.

THE TWENTY-FIRST CENTURY WHITE MANIFESTO

If you want to understand the current state of whiteness in America, you just have to read Jack Nicklaus's statement on Twitter from October 28, 2020. His statement personifies why 75 million Americans voted for Donald Trump, and I strongly believe it is a White manifesto for the twenty-first century:

Through the years, I have been blessed to personally know several Presidents on both sides of the aisle.

All were good people. All loved their country. And all believe in the American Dream.

I have had the privilege over the last 3½ years to get to know our current President a little more as his term has progressed. I have been very disappointed at what he's had to put up with from many directions, but with that, I have seen a resolve and a determination to do the right thing for our country. He has delivered on his promises. He's worked for the average person. In my opinion, he has been more diverse than any President I have seen and has tried to help people from all walks of life—equally.

I'm just a guy from Ohio and a Midwestern middle-class family, whose grandfathers both worked on the railroad. They gave their son, my father, the opportunity to pursue his education and his American Dream. I was taught strong family values and worked hard to pursue my own dreams, my own American Dream. I also believe that Donald Trump's policies will bring the American Dream to many families across the nation who are still trying to achieve it.

You might not like the way our President says or tweets some things, and trust me, I have told him that, but I have learned to look past that and focus on what he's tried to accomplish. This is not a personality contest; it's about patriotism, policies, and the people they impact. His love for America and its citizens, and putting his country first, has come through loud and clear. How he has said it has not been important to me. What has been important are his actions. Now, you have the opportunity to take action.

When Jack Nicklaus says there are "some things" that he is willing to overlook, those things include Donald Trump calling Black women dogs. They include calling African and Caribbean countries shit holes. They include willingly and wantonly allowing children from Mexico and Central America to be separated from their families at the border. He reduces Donald Trump's hatred and bigotry to two words: *some things*.

Jack Nicklaus was far from alone in not being bothered by Trump's bigotry, his removal of progressive district attorneys in favor of martial law, his sexism, the number of people in his administration who have been convicted of crimes and have gone to jail, or his telling the neofascist Proud Boys to "stand back and stand by" during the first debate with now President Joe Biden in September 2020.

For four years, Trump ignited every racial and cultural anxiety within White America and amplified these fears with his ongoing rallies, his blatant disrespect for members of the Democratic Party (particularly women of color within the party), and his refusal to condemn the race riot in Charlottesville, Virginia.

If you are a boxing fan, you know the sport has always pined for a "Great White Hope" since Jack Johnson became the first Black heavyweight boxing champion. Just look at the betting lines when Larry Holmes fought Gerry Cooney for the heavyweight title in June 1982. White America had their money on

Cooney; Black America stuck behind Holmes. When Harold Washington ran for mayor of Chicago in 1983, racist white Democrats were aghast when he beat two White candidates in the Democratic primary. He was supposed to coast to a victory. But when he faced White Republican challenger Bernard Epton, many White Democrats backed Epton. Washington won 51.7 percent to Epton's 48.0 percent, again, in a solidly Democratic city. Folks, when Donald Trump said only he could fix America, that was music to the ears of White GOP voters. He was their latest Great White Hope to continue creating the America that they've had for more than 400 years.

Many White Americans are now worried that they will no longer be the majority group in this country. From local broadcasts to cable news, no one can escape this pervasive White Fear that is constantly pushed through the media. White Americans can't seem to catch a break from the changing dynamics in the job market, increasing competition in higher education, more diversity in suburban areas, and the expanding population growth in minority and immigrant groups.

———

As we enter into this current decade, we are well on our way to America becoming a nation that is a majority of people of color, what some refer to as the emerging minority. When Donald

Trump declares that we need to "Make America Great Again!" he is referring to a time when this country was great for White Americans—but pure hell for people of color.

Recently, I read a story about a White man in Pennsylvania who wanted to go back to 1972 when his son graduated from college and wanted to get started with his first job. He said that he wished for the day when he could pick up the phone and guarantee that his son got a job. Could Black people do that in 1972? Hell no. When Donald Trump laments female reporters not being like actress Donna Reed, he's clearly hearkening back to a *Leave It to Beaver* America in which White men ruled the country; all women stayed home, raised the kids, and presided in the kitchen; and Black people were still under the vicious lash of Jim Crow in both the North and the South. This is the seemingly idyllic world that Donald Trump loves and adores—and this is exactly the world to which a significant number of White Americans want to return.

We have to look at the history of our country. We can't think that just because Black performer Darius Rucker received numerous awards at the Country Music Association Awards that we're all good and racial harmony pervades throughout the land. (When you take a closer look at the comments on the Country Music Association's social media accounts, it shows the real story of what's going on behind the scenes in America.)

We're doing a disservice to ourselves if, when we go home at the end of the day, we only associate with the same kind of people and never venture outside of our comfort zone to eat with other people, worship with other people, or understand the cultures and opinions of other people. We are living a lie every day if we don't acknowledge the truth of how we're living in this country.

DEFINING THE WHITE FEAR MANIFESTO

White Fear in the twenty-first century isn't just about terrorizing people of color with fire hoses and police dogs. It's now psychological warfare that makes White Americans believe vicious lies about their privilege, worth, and value in American society. In this section, I will break down how the White manifesto is continually being built on concepts of American superiority, the fierce opposition to the inclusion of people of color into the framework of American history, and the incredible backlash against the first Black president, Barack Obama.

CHAPTER FOUR

THE PROBLEM WITH PUTTING AMERICA FIRST

What are you without racism?

Are you any good?

Are you still strong?

Are you still smart? . . .

If you can only be tall because somebody else is on their knees, then you have a serious problem. And my feeling is that white people have a very, very serious problem, and they should start thinking about what THEY can do about it.

—Toni Morrison, interview with Charlie Rose, 1993

For more than forty years, blue-collar White men have been raked over the coals. The economy of twenty-first-century America has dwindled their paychecks, devalued their work, and closed down countless factories, mines, and shops throughout their communities. New scientific, medical, and technological industries began booming in cities where they didn't live and were powered by minority employees with advanced training and degrees that they didn't have. Many working-class White Americans believed that they were left behind during former President Obama's economic recovery efforts, and Trump's bloated promises to revive their jobs and restore quickly fading industries of a bygone era fueled White America's fight for survival.

Historically, why does this population believe that they are so underserved and disrespected? A significant part of this mental state is perpetuated by ideas of Northern states versus Southern states, big cities versus "real America," and the coastal states versus the "flyover" states. These have created an inferiority complex and an assumption that all the smart, rich, urbane, educated people look down on rural people. In other words, "Y'all look down on us and nobody likes us. The TV shows show us as backward hillbillies. We're portrayed as stupid, dumb hicks when we're not."

White Americans bought into this whole narrative. And, with the media and politicians defining the working class as White people in Rust Belt states, it's easy to see how the picture developed of average White Americans as the underdogs who care about family, faith, and hard work.

White psychology has been further shaped by the suffering livelihoods of White counties, cities, and states, from the once-unionized steel mills of Pennsylvania to the failing textile mills of Ohio to the struggling dairy and soybean farms in Iowa and Illinois. So then, the story of "the working class" becomes the story of Whiteness and the pursuit to hold onto the so-called American Dream. The next time you hear a politician talking about the "working class," they surely are not referring to people of color.

And about those jobs in the big cities? Most Black people have been locked out of those opportunities as well. There has been rampant racism that prevents Black Americans from gaining access to unionized jobs, purchasing their first homes, or investing in their children's educations.

As part of this discussion, you hear phrases such as "the heartland" and "the flyover states." Have you ever thought what these truly mean? Or what these people—the politicians and the media analysts—are talking about? They are indirectly talking about White America. Then, when you look at geography, you should also consider the Electoral College and how it has a lock on states such as Kansas, Nebraska, and Iowa, three extremely White states.

Let's go a step further and delve into how the predominantly White mass media works when reporting on working-class voters in various regions—this includes considering media traditionally defined as mainstream or defined as conservative.

When there are working-class conversations, do most of these media groups, no matter how they are defined, show Black people as working class? No, rarely. The justice system's targeting of nonworking Blacks, just like mass media, reinforce this bias by portraying welfare cases to be mostly nonworking Black people.

CONNECTING THE HISTORICAL
THREADS OF WHITE FEAR

In the past, we have looked at American history as two distinct periods: before the Civil War and after the Civil War. I believe this is a mistake. This demarcation doesn't acknowledge the continuation of racist policies and brutality against Black people after the war. All of these things are connected. We want to believe in a world in which the Civil War cured racism; however, the post-war years allowed White supremacy to continue for generations.

Dr. Martin Luther King, in a speech in 1965 at the conclusion of the Selma to Montgomery march, noted precisely what happened next: "To meet this threat, the southern aristocracy began immediately to engineer this development of a segregated society."

Newspapers saturated the thinking of the poor White masses and clouded their minds to the real issues of the Populist movement. Next, Southern White leaders created laws that made it a crime for Blacks and Whites to come together as equals anywhere.

These laws destroyed any opportunities for poor Whites and Blacks to join forces.

Dr. King closed that speech in 1965 by connecting the laws to the ballot, which allows us to better understand what we are faced with today:

> Thus, the threat of the free exercise of the ballot by the Negro and the white masses alike resulted in the establishment of a segregated society. They segregated southern money from the poor whites; they segregated southern mores from the rich whites; they segregated southern churches from Christianity; they segregated southern minds from honest thinking; and they segregated the Negro from everything. That's what happened when the Negro and white masses of the South threatened to unite and build a great society: a society of justice where none would prey upon the weakness of others; a society of plenty where greed and poverty would be done away; a society of brotherhood where every man would respect the dignity and worth of human personality . . .

Meanwhile, up north, the reformers of the Reconstruction destroyed the town of Wilmington, NC, because they were upset that too many Black people were in charge. The incomparable Ida B. Wells-Barnett courageously wrote about the mass number of lynchings that were taking place all over the South in the late nineteenth and early twentieth centuries, leading to her newspaper office in Memphis being destroyed and a massive bounty placed on her head. The 1921 decimation of the Greenwood Community in Tulsa, Oklahoma, was clearly an outcome of White economic fear.

In 1948, southern Democrats convened after the election of Harry Truman to make their feelings known to their opposition, the national party endorsing civil rights. One result of that meeting, eight years later, was the Southern Manifesto, also known as the 1956 Declaration of Constitutional Principles. The manifesto was also a probable reaction to *Brown v. Board of Education*. It was signed by many of the top political leaders from the South, who at the time held significant power in the U.S. Senate.

But what also came out of that was the reemergence of the Confederate flag. Rather than an act to honor the Confederate soldiers, this embrace of the flag was in reaction to Black people in America starting to garner economic and political power. For discouraged southern Whites, it was time for the second Civil War.

Brown v. Board of Education, the Civil Rights Act of 1964, the Voting Rights Act of 1965, and the Fair Housing Act of 1968 all further fueled White Fear. For instance, *Brown v. Board* happened in 1954 and most schools did not desegregate until the late 1960s and even as late as the 1970s. We are still dealing with the effects of the *Brown* decision today! So even with this landmark ruling, the echo of segregation lasted three generations, and even today our schools are not truly equal and integrated.

The idea that working-class people are White becomes a measure of the centuries-old North versus South arguments. But really, what it has evolved into is a view of Whiteness. Slavery has almost always been defined as a North-South rivalry. Yet White Americans in the North benefited economically from slavery. These economic advantages continued as land was settled during the pre-Civil war years of the 1800s through the westward movement and accumulation of territories. This includes the Compromise of 1820 as passed by Congress—Western territories south of the Missouri line were allowed to enslave, while those north of the line were prohibited—and the 1854 Kansas-Nebraska Act allowed settlers in those western territories to vote on the legality of enslavement.

In Kansas, pro-slavery militias, some of which can be considered the forerunner of militias in place today (including those involved in rioting at the Capitol in January 2021), attacked voters and stuffed ballot boxes in an attempt to ensure slavery would be legal in the new territories. This led to what became known as "Bleeding Kansas"—a major incident in the abolitionist movement. Finally, the Supreme Court's decision in the *Dred Scott v. Sandford* case of 1857 further intensified the debate of slavery in the western territories. Chief Justice Roger B. Taney wrote in the majority opinion that repealed the Missouri Compromise that because Black men and women were "beings on an inferior order" they had no right to Constitutional protections in the slave states and territories of the South and West. This decision buttressed the Fugitive Slave Act of 1850, which allowed paid "slave catchers" or bounty hunters (even Rangers, such as in Texas) to enter free states to capture "runaway slaves" and return them South to their "owners." The entire American economy was built on this notion of slavery that created the foundation for American capitalism. The need to dominate Black people continued after the Civil War and following the demise of Reconstruction, becoming a major facet of the post-Reconstruction policies of Jim Crow, which solidified the repression and nonpayment of Black workers. Again, our politics have always been about appealing to the White American worker.

Let's check the speech Dr. Martin Luther King Jr. gave on March 25, 1965, at his "Address at the Conclusion of the Selma to Montgomery March," as it has formally become known. Remember it. It has elements that most people have glossed over, ignored, minimized, while emphasizing other things he said that day. But don't be mistaken—some of the things Dr. King said that day are among the most salient in this, the most powerful of all the speeches he made. Dr. King said with power:

> Now it is not an accident that one of the great marches of American history should terminate in Montgomery, Alabama. Just ten years ago, in this very city, a new philosophy was born of the Negro struggle. Montgomery was the first city in the South in which the entire Negro community united

and squarely faced its age-old oppressors. Out of this struggle, more than bus [de]segregation was won; a new idea, more powerful than guns or clubs was born. Negroes took it and carried it across the South in epic battles that electrified the nation and the world.

This was only part of the slow build, as he described what occurred over the years and decades, coming to the real emphasis to remember from that day, for how the nation had even arrived at this distorted point of racism and separation through the years of Jim Crow. He continued:

> Our whole campaign in Alabama has been centered around the right to vote. In focusing the attention of the nation and the world today on the flagrant denial of the right to vote, we are exposing the very origin, the root cause, of racial segregation in the Southland. Racial segregation as a way of life did not come about as a natural result of hatred between the races immediately after the Civil War. There were no laws segregating the races then.
>
> As the noted historian C. Vann Woodward in his book *The Strange Career of Jim Crow* clearly points out, the segregation of the races was really *a political stratagem employed by the emerging financial interests in the South to keep the southern masses divided and southern labor the cheapest in the land.*

You see, it was a simple thing to keep the poor white masses working for near-starvation wages in the years that followed the Civil War. Why, if the poor White plantation or mill worker became dissatisfied with his low wages, the plantation or mill owner would merely threaten to fire him and hire former Negro slaves and pay him even less. Thus, the southern wage level was kept almost unbearably low.

By keeping White Southern laborers under the illusion that they were slightly better off than their Black counterparts, the Southern plantation owners could continue financially pillaging both Black and White laborers with few consequences and larger profits.

WEAPONIZING THE WORKING-CLASS VOTER

Consider when the average White American says, "I can't stand identity politics." Identity politics means that you are campaigning toward a particular identity. But the reality is that the notion of the working class is identity politics because messaging then begins to revolve around that.

One of my biggest criticisms of Senator Bernie Sanders was how he used the phrase "working class." While it sounded fresh and new to millennials and Gen Z voters, Bernie was essentially voicing the same rhetoric that centered around Whiteness. When Bernie kept saying, "We've got to target the working class," ask yourself, "Is the working class about income? Is the working class based on industry and employment? Is it based on location?"

Because if you actually go back and look at the numbers, most working-class Americans did not vote for Donald Trump.

Most media reports claimed Trump had energized and empowered potential working-class voters with his brash, unapologetic style and unforgiving takes on hot-button issues. Because Trump stirred up this group in a way that many of them had never been stirred before, they came out in full force, first to his political rallies and then to the voting booth. But while this story sounds convincing, it's actually not true.

The average Trump voter is actually very much in alignment with the traditional Republican voting base. Working-class Americans fit into this narrative but not at the rate and pace as depicted in the media. For example, in 2016, Hillary Clinton earned more votes from working-class voters than Trump, further illustrating that Democrats still have a healthier stronghold with working-class Americans overall.

When pollsters and polling organizations say working class, that's a euphemism for White people. Middle-class White people. Then, mainstream media picks up on that when they aren't being very specific. Trump isn't appealing to all of the working class—he's appealing to the White working class.

For instance, the *Harvard Business Review* article "How Biden Won Back (Enough of) the White Working Class" cites that the percentage of White working-class men voting Democrat increased from 23 percent to 28 percent, while White working-class women's support for Democrats increased from 34 percent to 36 percent. That means that Donald Trump received 72 percent of the White working-class male vote and he won 64 percent of the White female working-class vote.

So, the problem is when the phrase "the working-class voter" is used, the media lazily doesn't identify these working-class people as White. We have to unpack this phraseology of working class because, in most cases, they are talking about White working-class people—and not factoring in working-class people of color.

What has occurred since the period of Bourbon Democrats (business interests) and the end of the Populist movement is that the division between White and Black workers has grown more severe. Broke White people have always needed a scapegoat for their problems. Unfortunately, they never understood that the scapegoat for their problems were the idiotic politicians for whom they kept voting who kept screwing them, as well as the business interests who don't want to pay them fair wages. That story that King told, which has been the case ever since then, is these poor Whites are always blaming Black people for their problems.

If they can't get a job, it's because of "them"—Blacks and others of color. It's because of affirmative action. "I can't get promoted because of them." It's always "them." It's never "I can't read, I need more education." It's never "I didn't go to school." It's never "I want to be White and live in this small town, where my parents have lived, my grandparents have lived, but the manufacturing facility shut down and there are no jobs." It's like they're thinking, "I'm watching TV and I'm seeing LeBron James, and I'm seeing Oprah, I'm seeing Tiger, and I'm seeing these rappers, and look at all these Black people having these great lives," and they want to conclude that their own unhappiness is *their* fault, these Black people.

This is what happens all throughout American history—especially since Jim Crow—and it really took off when Democrats embraced civil rights in the 1960s. White people began to form this view of "you all are doing too much for them." It never dawned on them that they'd always had an advantage.

But then, when you look at the data, though Black people were assumed to have been overwhelmingly aided by President Lyndon Johnson's war on poverty, in fact, just like after slavery, the standards of living of Whites increased because the war on poverty helped White people. There are more White people on food stamps than there are Blacks. There are more White people on welfare. There are more White people being assisted with housing.

Certainly, many Blacks were assisted by the war on poverty policies because they were disproportionately poor. But there were more White people in America who were poor. So, remember, the narrative of poor has never been White. The narrative of poor became Black. The face of poverty became Black. Even though the whole time, the numbers, the statistics, were showing more White people in poverty in the United States. Now the narrative of the working class has become a powerful political weapon.

CHAPTER FIVE

REDEFINING AMERICAN HISTORY

*If we start changing our way of life to accommodate [them] . . .
there is nowhere for us to go.*

These words were uttered in 2015 by a member of the St.
Cloud, Minnesota, city council who was attempting to block
legal immigrants from Somalia from coming into the community.
With White American birth rates sharply declining and White
American death rates quickly increasing due to poor health and
the opioid crisis, many White Americans are terrified by the
prospect of becoming extinct in their own country, similar to
what we have witnessed in many European nations.

In a rally in Minnesota in 2016, Trump victoriously
responded, "You have seen firsthand the problems caused with
faulty refugee vetting, with large numbers of Somali refugees

coming into your state, without your knowledge, without your support or approval. You've suffered enough, Minnesota."

Donald Trump's entire presidency was based on pushing racial buttons. It's no coincidence that Critical Race Theory became an issue at the forefront of White Fear after the 2020 election. The Republican Party needed this issue to stoke White Fear for the 2022 midterm and 2024 presidential election. The powers that be need White people to be upset and bothered.

While Donald Trump stoked the flames, the issue of White Fear continues to evolve beyond him. The year 2043, when America will become a majority-minority nation, is just over two decades away. White Americans are now reckoning with understanding that they will no longer be able to define the history and the future of this country through the prism of Whiteness. While they have determined everything from beauty standards to generational wealth to the political process, they now have to view America from the vantage point of people of color—and having to share their view of America is driving them insane.

White America is now using Critical Race Theory as a boogeyman term to refer to any discussion in school about the history of systemic racism in America and the contemporary reality of ongoing systemic racism. They simply do not want that analysis provided. They don't have a rebuttal to it other than to just say, "Well, there's no racism because Obama won." But truth be told, if it were up to White folks, Obama wouldn't have won.

Most White Americans in 2008 were happier with the prospect of Sarah Palin becoming president than Barack Obama. So how are you going to hold up progress when you weren't part of it? How are you going to brag about the progress we've made and then put on a hat that says, "Make America Great Again," which means you don't think we needed to make all that progress because you agreed with how America was seventy years ago? The contradictions are massive.

The fact is that no Democratic president has won the White House with a majority of White voters since Lyndon Baines Johnson. Bill Clinton got 49 percent of the White vote in 1992. In 2008, Barack Obama got 43 percent. This is vital to understand because regardless of all the talk about minority voters, White voters constituted at least 72 percent of those casting ballots in 2020.

Including Critical Race Theory upsets the whitewashed version of history we've always been taught, a version that omits the true nature of the way this country was founded. And it ignores the fact that we are still fighting for basic civil rights to this day.

We prefer the George Washington and the cherry tree history, even though that story was a lie. George Washington didn't cut down a cherry tree and run and tell his daddy. George Washington barely knew his daddy. His daddy died when George was young. That's all a made-up story, but we prefer that to the truth that George Washington was a particularly vicious enslaver of other human beings who, when they made the mistake of running away from Mount Vernon, had them tracked down and took bounties out on them.

Now, if you don't want me to say that because that's unpatriotic, your problem is not with political correctness but with historical accuracy. For years, White America has been able to ignore the truth. Now the culture and the demographics are such that White Americans are having to confront the things that they have tried to deny—and for some folks it's too painful to look at. But, if it's painful to look at, imagine how much more painful it's been for Black and Brown folks to live through it in this country.

For every White American who is watching Sean Hannity, Laura Ingraham, and Tucker Carlson each evening and then petitioning their school boards to remove Critical Race Theory from their district's curriculum, this rally cry ultimately boils down to their fear and anger about Black people, Latino people, and Asian people now having an opinion about what it means to be an American.

If White Americans can't even accept that Black people were oppressed in the fictional book *To Kill a Mockingbird*, which is about racism in Alabama in the mid-1930s, how will we expect them to see the reality of America as it is unfolding in the twenty-first century?

At the end of the Trump Administration, there was a visceral and vitriolic reaction to the adoption of the 1619 Project coming into American classrooms. The 1619 Project was a multi-part series in the *New York Times* spearheaded by Nikole Hannah-Jones that documented the Black experience in America from the arrival of the first enslaved Africans in Jamestown, Virginia.

To have the president of the United States tweeting his anger about this project being included in American history classrooms during the middle of a global pandemic was absolutely ridiculous. But Trump's unfounded outrage speaks to the larger issue of White Americans' fear and fury about no longer being the sole voice in determining what constitutes American history.

White Americans have controlled the entire apparatus. They've controlled the narrative, the media, and the academic instruction behind American history. Now they are being forced to accept more stories outside of the dominant narrative of colonialism and Christian values.

REINTERPRETING WHITE AMERICAN SYMBOLISM

Let's go back in history for a moment. After the Civil War, it was agreed that the Rebel flag that represented the Confederate Army was problematic as a symbol of the great division as a result of the war. The Rebel flag had all but disappeared for two generations after the Civil War.

Then in 1948, the national Democratic Party made an appeal to Black voters by including a civil rights plank in their platform. That so angered the white racist southern Dixiecrats that they convened a meeting in Mississippi and formed their own wing of the party in order to continue to advance racial segregation. It was at this point when the Confederate flag began to reemerge in American society. From that point on, it remained the defining symbol of those opposed to racial equality. Then there was the renaming of schools after Confederate generals. Next, there was the rewriting and redefining of the Civil War—rebranded The Lost Cause or The War of Northern Aggression—to avoid history making it clear the war was caused by the South's refusal to give up slavery. Whiteness has to be asserted at all times.

When Black advancement gained traction after the Civil Rights Movement, the response to integrated housing led to White flight, which led to the growth of the suburbs. The economic system allowed Whites to freeze Black people out of certain neighborhoods. Then there was White backlash on affirmative action and the inclusion of quotas. White Americans in the corporate environment were perfectly fine with Black people being in apprenticeships or entry-level positions but balked at them as managing directors, executive vice presidents, or CEOs.

This same backlash against diversity continued through the 1980s and the dawning of PC culture.

American values are not to be messed with. We expect everyone to salute the flag, enjoy high school football on Friday nights, and finish off their meal with a slice of hot apple pie. If you don't adhere to these values, you're disrespecting the very ideals that many White Americans have built their entire lives on. White Fear is stoked every day in this country when a person of color pushes back on patriotic values and questions the execution of our democracy.

––––––––––

There's nothing more American than sitting down on a Sunday with a beer and an afternoon of football. But when Black and Brown athletes dare do anything outside of running a ball, they are an immediate threat to White America. It's okay for athletes to nearly break their bodies on the field, but why is it an outrage when those same athletes protest the breaking of Black and Brown bodies all across this country? Why is it a problem for athletes to use their platforms to bring awareness to the problems that continue to plague communities of color?

Black athletes have been standing in resistance to White Fear throughout the history of this country. White America has no problem with Michael Jordan winning six NBA championships for the Chicago Bulls or Simone Biles winning an Olympic gold medal in gymnastics or Tiger Woods winning more than eighty golf tournaments. But the minute these Black and Brown athletes start speaking out about what's going on in urban communities, suddenly they no longer give a damn about how many yards you can run or how many baskets you can score.

It was no surprise, then, when Donald Trump viciously spoke out against the NFL and Colin Kaepernick in the fall of 2017. He spoke directly to the core of White American values. Most White Americans equate the American flag and "The Star-Spangled Banner" as keystones of American patriotism. Anyone who dares to defile or challenge the flag is automatically deemed as anti-American. White Americans don't care if we are getting our asses kicked in the street or being gunned down by police. Their thoughts can be summed up as, "I don't care what you ni—s are going through. You're all going to salute that damn flag." In 2016, when San Francisco 49er quarterback Colin Kaepernick knelt during the national anthem, it felt like a direct threat to American values.

Long before Kaepernick, baseball legend Jackie Robinson spoke to the same challenges that are still going on right now. In his memoir, *I Never Had It Made*, Robinson wrote:

> There I was the black grandson of a slave, the son of a black sharecropper, part of a historic occasion, a symbolic hero to my people. The air was sparkling. The sunlight was warm. The band struck up the national anthem. The flag billowed in the wind. It should have been a glorious moment for me as

the stirring words of the national anthem poured from the stands. Perhaps it was, but then again perhaps the anthem could be called the theme song for a drama called The Noble Experiment. Today as I look back on that opening game of my first world series, I must tell you that it was Mr. Rickey's drama and that I was only a principal actor. As I write this twenty years later, I cannot stand and sing the anthem. I cannot salute the flag; I know that I am a black man in a white world. In 1972, in 1947, at my birth in 1919, I know that I never had it made.

We can look back a little further and see the bold resistance of Jesse Owens when he defied Adolph Hitler during the 1936 Olympics in Munich. Despite his athletic and patriotic efforts, President Franklin Delano Roosevelt refused to extend Owens an invitation to the White House.

Or, what about prominent Black athletes such as Tommie Smith and John Carlos, who faced severe backlash and even death threats after giving the Black Power salute during the 1968 Olympics in Mexico, or boxing legend Muhammad Ali being banned from the ring for three years for protesting the war in Vietnam?

Beyond the sports arenas, Black newspaper owners, editors, and writers were threatened with treason during World War II because they were writing about the racism that Black soldiers were facing in the armed forces. White folks responded with

"This is not the time for that. We don't care what you are going through. There's a war going on."

So, Donald Trump knew exactly what he was doing by attacking Kaepernick and any other NFL player who defied the American flag. American values have always been more valuable than Black and Brown bodies. A White person can look at Kaepernick and say, "How dare you not stand for and salute the American flag! This is disrespectful to our military members and our first responders." But these same people do not want to accept the reality of cops who continue to commit brutalities under the color of the law and with an American flag on their uniforms.

There are a significant number of White Americans who simply don't care. They don't give a damn about children being kept in cages at the borders. They don't care about Trump's hundreds of thousands of lies that he's told over the four years of his presidency. They don't care that he's given over the Department of the Interior and the EPA to the oil and gas industries. They don't care that his tax cut actually benefited the wealthy and completely screwed middle and lower classes. They don't care that he routinely insulted women. They overlook all of that because they are too afraid of the Black and Brown train that is coming their way.

In 2019, the journalist and political analyst Ron Brownstein tweeted, "Whatever you consider the merits of #impeachment, the image of an endless procession of angry white & preponderantly male Republican legislators railing bitterly against a diverse Democratic caucus offers a chilling preview of how our politics may evolve as US grows more diverse."

But as the country begins to undergo this demographic shift, these White values no longer get to dictate and determine everything. These White values are no longer the dominant worldview. White people in America are having to deal with the reality that the world they created, their safe suburban dream, is no longer going to be the way we live in this country. The reality of a swiftly changing America is here and now.

For decades, people of color have had to deal with being called racial slurs, being told to stop speaking their native language, being forced to change their hair or not to wear any cultural garb, and essentially being forced to change their entire cultural perspective to be acceptable in this country.

As America transforms into amassing numbers of Black people and other people of color, we are demanding more power positions, more seats at the table, and more access to the C-suites. We are no longer settling for being relegated to certain neighborhoods to keep White people comfortable. We are demanding that you share the resources and that you see us as equals. As the reality of the country shifting to a majority-minority country looms largely, our worldview will now have an opportunity to be seen, valued, and appreciated.

White America is so used to being able to silence Black and Brown people and not have to consider their views. They are used to sprinkling their view a little bit or just seasoning the dominant narrative with some views from the outside. But Black folks are now saying, "No, we're going to actually teach our view regardless of what you think. We're going to study the 1619 Project and redefine the actual founding and the origins of the country," which is not displacing the dominant narrative but saying you have to also consider another perspective. But if you've never had to do that before, it feels like the end of the world. It is the definition of fragility. It is the definition of "snowflake" behavior.

The question is, are we going to just remember the fictional version of American history? Or are we going to be honest that the country has been foundationally built on a contradiction? Are we going to rest on the promise of democracy or the reality of oppression? Are we going to be honest that modern-day American democracy only benefits the few and marginalizes the rest of the country? If you can't deal with that as a White American, then you're proving that this country is less emotionally mature than countries all around the world that have done a far better job at confronting their history.

The Germans, South Africans, post-apartheid, and Rwandans, after their genocide, have all done a better job at confronting and reckoning with their history. Here we are in America hundreds of years later and we're still so consumed with the need to be the greatest country ever that we're not willing to look at the real damage that has been done, which ultimately means that we can't move forward as a nation. If you can't confront that pain and that past, you cannot move into the future as a proud and confident nation and a pluralistic democracy.

Many White folks never have to think about the issue of White supremacy as a system and its role in their own lives. The problem is the only way you get better at it is to challenge your family, challenge your colleagues, and talk to your children. If you're a White child, talk to your parents. Sometimes the children are ahead of the parents in that regard and ask real fundamental questions, such as "How did this church get to be so White?" or "How did this school get to be so White?" or "Why is this neighborhood so White?" There are lots of places to start, but you have to start somewhere if you're going to thoughtfully discuss racial issues and gain insight.

THE CRITICAL RACE THEORY UMBRELLA

In 2021, the Texas Senate voted to pass a bill that would eliminate the requirement that public schools teach that the Ku Klux Klan is morally wrong. That same bill dropped studying Martin Luther King Jr.'s "I Have a Dream" speech as a curriculum requirement. In Oklahoma, they passed an emergency rule on House Bill 1775, banning Critical Race Theory—and it wasn't

even being taught in Oklahoma schools. Other rules implemented included a stipulation that parents are permitted to
inspect school curriculum and teachers who violate rules could
face suspension. White conservatives are going nuts. They're
trying to group everything they oppose under Critical Race Theory, and it's idiotic.

In 2021, there were commemorations for and media spe-
cials on the centennial of the Tulsa Race Massacre in 1921.
This spotlight on our history ushered in a new era of grappling
with the truth of this horrific moment in American history,
and school districts would have the opportunity to adopt new
curriculum (yet it wasn't until 2021 that the state of Oklahoma
required the race riot to be taught in its schools). Beyond the
implications of finally teaching young people in this country
the truth about Tulsa, this was also an opportunity for Black
folks to deal with questions such as, "Where would African
Americans be in terms of generational wealth if this original
community had survived?"

While many Americans were curious and eager to learn more
about this slice of American history, there was an immediate cry
in White America about making students feel uncomfortable.
Making a student feel uncomfortable, to feel anguish or guilt, is
a small price to pay while showing the full scope in the American experience. It's outrageous that teaching this history could
result in potential penalties of teachers losing their teaching

certificates and, even further, a school district losing accreditation, which means losing all of its state funding.

Actor Tom Hanks perfectly addressed the topic in his *New York Times* editorial in June 2021:

> For a white kid living in the white neighborhoods of Oakland, Calif., my city in the 1960s and '70s looked integrated and diverse but often felt tense and polarized, as was evident on many an AC Transit bus. The division between white America and Black America seemed to be as solid as any international boundary even in one of the most integrated cities in the nation.
>
> The truth about Tulsa, and the repeated violence by some white Americans against Black Americans, was systematically ignored, perhaps because it was regarded as too honest, too painful a lesson for our young white ears.
>
> How different would perspectives be had we all been taught about Tulsa in 1921, even as early as the fifth grade? Today, I find the omission tragic, an opportunity missed, a teachable moment squandered.

The education bill that was ratified in Oklahoma doesn't specify "Critical Race Theory" in its wording. It says that you can't talk about meritocracy or speak about hard-work ethic being related to somebody's race or identity. It further states that you can't make people feel anguish, guilt, or any type of fear in regard to their race or their gender. There's coded language in there, but underneath all of it is the ability to silence conversations about race, to silence conversations about the truth in our history.

There are so many things that are attached to the fear that is surrounding these bills in Texas and Oklahoma and more bills that will continue to come long after I finish writing this book. When we finally try to speak the truth and put that in the standards, it's three steps forward and four steps back. These White leaders do not want race; they don't want diversity; they don't want any of this stuff being taught; and their strategy is to put everything under this Critical Race Theory umbrella.

This is why there has been so much opposition to the 1619 Project and other efforts to re-examine American history. When we talk about issues of racial inequality, whether it be economic inequality, inequality in education, or inequality in the criminal justice system, White America just wants to pretend that today is today and we have no past. They want to pretend that there's no long history and legacy of legalized discrimination. White America wants to use that rhetoric of equality without actually having to do anything to address the inequality. If you actually have to grapple with the past and all of the institutions that really conspired to keep Black people in the lower caste, then you are charged with having to do something to rectify the current inequality. We have to exist in this space where the only thing that matters about our past are the good things and all of the bad things about our past are irrelevant to the society we live in today.

But as Black, Latino, Indigenous, and Asian Americans, we cannot allow ourselves to be baited into having arguments that don't serve the work that we're trying to do. The very same people who were outraged about the estate of Dr. Seuss taking six books out of print for racist content and connotation are the same people who are applauding efforts by Republican lawmakers all across America to prohibit the teaching of the 1619 Project. We have to understand what the actual strategy is here, so that we can correctly push back. Having arguments about cancel culture and culture wars are really useless. We have to stop using euphemisms and call this out for what it is. We don't have time to debate the existence of slavery or its continued effects on Black people throughout this nation. Instead, we have to focus on political polices that continue to perpetuate systemic racism. White Fear can no longer define the parameters of this conversation about our history.

CHAPTER SIX

THE AUDACITY OF OBAMA

There's a scene in the movie *The Good Shepherd* that essentially reimagines the CIA trying to get the mafia to kill Fidel Castro. The mobster played by Joe Pesci says at one point, "We Italians, we got our families, and we got the church; the Irish, they have the homeland, Jews their tradition; even the niggers, they got their music. What about you people, Mr. Wilson, what do you have?"

Matt Damon's character replies, "The United States of America. The rest of you are just visiting."

If there is any scene in Hollywood history that adequately encapsulates America, it is this one. It sums up the attitude of this nation from its founding to present day.

The rise of Donald Trump in 2016 was clearly a referendum on the audacity of Barack Obama becoming the first Black president. When Barack Obama took office on January 20, 2009, he sparked two things throughout the nation—he simultaneously represented the future possibilities of this country and the fear of a changing America.

Just weeks before the 2016 election, a former New Jersey police chief who was on trial for slamming a Black teenager's head into a doorjamb reportedly called Donald Trump "The last hope for White people." While this officer was eventually charged with a hate crime, we can clearly see how Donald Trump's candidacy emboldened White racists to come out of the closet and become dangerously brazen with their actions.

President Obama's election made a lot of White America wake up to the reality that the country was headed in a new direction and this change was not going to go down easy.

In his book, *We Were Eight Years in Power*, writer Ta-Nehesi Coates perfectly articulated how Obama appealed to White voters and solidified this comfort in his presidency for two terms:

Although we're perceived to be different Obama pushed that citizens were connected by a common dream. Obama appealed to a belief in innocence—in particular white innocence—that ascribed the country's historical errors more to misunderstanding . . . than to any deliberate malevolence or widespread racism. This appeal attracted people because it allowed them to feel that America was good. Entertaining this idea of white innocence was a matter of political survival. Whenever he attempted to buck this directive, he was disciplined.

Obama's successful run and election was a radical juxtaposition to the 1984 and 1988 presidential campaigns of the Reverend Jesse Jackson. Even though his policies and platform were strong, Jesse Jackson was an undeniable threat to White Americans. There were jokes in the Jackson campaign about how low they could cut his hair to make him more appealing to White America. It didn't matter that he was an ordained minister or that his organizations provided food and economic resources to thousands of people throughout Chicago. White America couldn't fathom letting him get anywhere near the White House.

When Obama mounted his first campaign nearly twenty years later, this Harvard-educated lawyer with a Princeton-educated wife and two daughters were more palatable to White America. As qualified and talented as Obama was, the overriding factor was how he would appeal to White Americans, because rule number one is that we always have to cater to how White America feels. Even with all of that safeness, Obama still unleashed an underbelly of White Fear for the next eight years. White Americans are not going to react well to a call for equality in their America.

Barely one year into Obama's presidency, when the American Survey Center issued a survey on Americans' optimism about the future of the country, overwhelmingly White Americans noted that they felt more fearful and less hopeful for the future and the fate of their children.

But if you would ask that same White American if he would correlate his fear to racism, he would rebut, "How can you accuse America of being racist? We just elected Barack Obama!" The default stance in America is that racism is no longer an issue because we elected the first Black president and later the first Black vice president. My response would be that Thurgood Marshall's appointment to the Supreme Court did not end racism in the criminal justice system. President Truman's desegregation of the armed forces did not eradicate discrimination in the military. This is the ongoing dichotomy of race in this country that will never end.

In our history, Black success has been followed by White backlash. Examples of Black people rising, getting ahead, and demanding equality kicks White Fear into gear. We saw it after Reconstruction when the first Black senators were elected to Congress in the 1870s. After they were removed from office, it would be another 100 years before another Black person was elected to the Senate from the South. We saw it in New York City with the victory of Rudy Giuliani after the election of the city's first Black mayor, David Dinkins. So the rise of Donald Trump was certainly not a surprise to Black America.

Republicans will argue that their responses to Obama's policies were purely based on political differences and that it had nothing to do with race. But when you look at Republican Congressman Joe Wilson screaming, "You lie!" to Obama in 2009, that was clearly White Fear. When you factor in Franklin Graham continuing to cast doubt on Obama being a Christian, essentially saying he was secretly a Black Muslim, that was White Fear at its finest. And when you consider the GOP blocking Obama's nomination of Merrick Garland to the Supreme Court nine months before the end of his term, yet turning around and appointing Amy Coney Barrett less than two months before the 2020 election, that's White Fear *and* hypocrisy . . . two for the price of one.

When you examine the Democratic presidencies of Jimmy Carter and Bill Clinton, both successful Southern governors, even they had to find ways to appeal to deeply loyal White Republicans to get to the White House. In Jon Ward's book *Camelot's End: The Democrats' Last Great Civil War*, he described how during Carter's run for governor of Georgia and his 1976 campaign for president, he had to appeal to White racists and get them comfortable with this picture of him being the son of peanut farmers and looking out for the common man. Bill Clinton's 1992 campaign had to include language about being tough on crime so that White Americans could see his ability to be tough on the Black community.

Trump's rise to the presidency was also fueled by the idea that the country was not doing enough for White Americans. Thomas Edsall wrote in the *New York Times* that McComb County,

Mississippi, voted for Obama in both 2008 and 2012, but in 2016, it overwhelmingly voted for Donald Trump. Many of the exit polls in McComb County showed the same data from voters in 1980 during the election of Ronald Reagan: "I voted for Reagan because Walter Mondale and the Democrats are doing too much for the Blacks." Edsall wrote that 25 to 28 percent of voters in this county in 2016 were deeply distraught with Obamacare, the Marriage Equality Act, and other big government programs that they felt left them out in the cold. When a quarter of your voting block believes that Washington hasn't lived up to expectations, you can then run a successful campaign based on White Fear.

YOU CAN'T SEPARATE TRUMP AND THE REPUBLICAN PARTY

With a Democrat back in the White House in 2021 with President Joe Biden, it was easy for the nation to fall under a false sense of security, assuming we'd eradicated the insanity that was the Trump presidency. This was the mistake Hillary Clinton made in 2016. She tried to separate Trump from the Republican Party. The issue is not Donald Trump. Donald Trump is simply their standard-bearer. The issue is that they're still in power. Separating Donald Trump from the Republican Party and their policies and their racism and their White nationalism simply allows them to move Trump out while retaining the White nationalists.

The issue is that the Republican Party is the leader of White Fear, which is fueled on by Fox News, One America News, and Newsmax. Unless you deal with the racists, unless you deal with them being in power, nothing is going to change.

The Republican Party is in a laboratory where they create different versions of today's White nationalist party. In the lab, they also created Donald Trump. Donald Trump was so nasty, so vicious, so lethal, and he was accidentally released. But he still was the creation and the manifestation of the party, so they supported him. But now they want a quieter, nicer version of Donald Trump with the same White nationalist policies. You can't mistakenly believe "if only Donald Trump was gone, we're good." No, the Republican Party is still going to be appealing to the White nationalists.

No dentist allows some rotten decay to stay in your mouth. It's going to infect your other teeth. You can't have a partial root canal. You have to have a complete root canal. You can't partially remove a brain tumor. You cannot declare yourself cancer free if there's cancer still in your body.

For us to move forward, there has to be a 24/7 focus of completely removing the decay, removing the cancer, removing the evil. And the Republican Party has decided, "We're not going to do that." The evil, the decay, the cancer, Trump is still there. Those who agree with him are still there. They are still in power. Those who voted not to accept the electors are still in power. So we are still at war.

In the summer of 2021, Peter Wehner summed up the post-Trump Republican party in the *Atlantic* as follows:

> Republicans who assumed that the party would return to sanity after Trump left office never understood how deforming the effects of his presidency would be. For many, Trump's behaviors were initially a bug; eventually, they became a feature. Republicans ignored his corruptions and reveled in his cruelty. To better understand what's happening in the GOP, think of a person with an addiction who over time develops a tolerance. As a result, they need more potent and more frequent doses of the drug to get their desired high. And sometimes even that isn't enough.

During the 1988 presidential campaign, then-Republican candidate George H. W. Bush surged in the polls by scaring White voters with the image of a Black inmate named Willie Horton breaking into their homes and taking advantage of their women. Twenty years later during the 2008 Democratic Primary Debate, then-Senator Joe Biden astonishingly and condescendingly told the soon-to-be President Barack Obama that he spoke so well and intelligently.

It doesn't take a genius to sniff out Donald Trump's agenda. From refusing to denounce White supremacists in Charlottesville, Virginia, to insulting late civil rights legend and Representative John Lewis and his district to calling African and

Caribbean countries "shitholes" to demanding that four female representatives who were born on U.S. soil to "go back to their native countries," we know what a backlash on the American Dream sounds like—and this administration held no punches in making their intentions clear in destroying the hopes and dreams of Black America.

The question is no longer whether Donald Trump is a racist. We now have to ask why was it okay for the President of the United States to use the White House as his personal bully pulpit. We have to ask why we settled for a new normal in which the president could shout threats from Twitter and then send out his minions to defend his vitriol on the Sunday news shows.

We are living in a time where we can no longer afford to avoid the truth. That means that White folks are going to have to start listening for these dog whistles and begin calling out other White folks.

The next twenty-five years will move us toward one of the greatest racial transformations that we've ever had in this country. But we have to know what this really means. We can't just focus on voter suppression, redistricting, or the fight around illegal immigration. We have to get down to the nuts and bolts of racial inequality and force White people to change their ways, behaviors, and viewpoints.

White Fear became more severe with Black mayors rising into power in the 1970s and 1980s. Great politicians such as Maynard

Jackson in Atlanta, Coleman Young in Detroit, and Harold Washington in Chicago were challenging the ideals of American leadership. They were demanding more jobs, fair housing, and equal access for Black and Brown people. We felt this collective anger from White America that said, "Hold up, now. You can't take what belongs to us!"

Politicians stoked White Fear even further by running campaigns with slogans such as "Vote for me before it's too late." White people began fleeing major American cities by the thousands. You saw White people in Boston viciously opposing busing Black children to predominantly White schools.

The difference now is that we're not telling people they have to change—the numbers are now dictating the story. These changes in the American demographic are happening right before our very eyes, and they are going to continue unfolding whether White America likes it or not.

Every day the news is flooded with constant messages asking, "How do we slow this thing down?" or "How do we stop immigrants from spilling across our borders?" But White America can't stop this evolution. White America is now being forced to deal with something that they have no control over: their loss of dominance and control. Can you just imagine how frightening and unsettling this is to a race of people who are so used to being in complete control? It's no wonder Donald Trump is still holding rallies to keep his base fired up.

Now White America is going to have to face the fact that soon their opinions won't matter as much. They are going to have to deal with the swell of energized voters who are fed up with White America clinging to power that will no longer be theirs to control. It's time for White folks to examine who they are and understand that they are going to have to make changes. They are going to have to confront their past and stand in the truth of who they are right now.

Black America can hear the howls of resistance from White America loud and clear. These hit dogs are hollering, and we must take our attention from this inane barking and bite back with concrete strategies and implementation to move America forward out of this nightmare of nonsense.

SECTION THREE

LEGISLATING AND REGULATING THROUGH WHITE FEAR

If you can't impose White Fear at the grassroots level, there's no better way to keep Black people down than to impose legal measures that subjugate and terrorize people of color and keep them out of the American Dream for generations. In this section, I will walk you through the challenges of White Fear through the American judicial system and the voting booth.

CHAPTER SEVEN

HOW WHITE FEAR TERRORIZES THE AMERICAN JUDICIARY

During the Trump administration, Mitch McConnell was ready, willing, and eager to enact his plan to fill as many federal and Supreme Court nominations as possible. During the Obama administration he had blocked more than 100 judges, and of course he blocked Obama's final nominee, Merrick Garland, for nine months before the end of his second term. McConnell had his eyes set on filling up the courts with as many young, White, mostly male conservative judges as possible. For Whiteness to be maintained, the courts were now the prime focus of the Republican Party.

Why do you think Mitch McConnell had been so hell bent on approving as many conservative judges as possible? It's because he could clearly see the day when America will no longer be a majority White nation. By the end of Trump's term, the U.S. Senate had confirmed a total of 226 federal judges, confirmed 174 district court judges, fifty-four appellate court judges, and three conservative Supreme Court Justices, Neil Gorsuch, Brett Kavanaugh, and Amy Coney Barrett. Eighty-five percent of the judges appointed by Trump have been White and 76 percent were men.

These judicial confirmations were huge wins for Donald Trump, McConnell, and White, right-wing conservative evangelicals. Nan Aron, the president of the progressive group Alliance for Justice, said, "They're stacking the courts with individuals who will rule with them in lockstep on their agenda." In chapter eight I will go into greater detail about how this radical right reshaping of the judicial system is yet another tool to maintain a White majority by creating a conservative agenda, blocking liberal policies, and shutting down progressive legislation for people of color.

When Trump became president, McConnell then had the power to fill all of the judicial positions that he blocked during the Obama administration, and he effectively empowered Trump to appoint 25 percent of the judges that came onto the bench during Trump's four years in office. The rationale of controlling the courts for the Republican Party is that politicians will come and go, but federal laws and rulings will stay. The courts are the final arbiter of the law, and if you have the right judges in place, any law that you deem fit will become the law of the land. To maintain power, the courts are an essential part of maintaining the rule of White America.

Republicans were purposefully looking for judges between the ages of thirty-five and forty-five to declare the rule of Whiteness across the land for as long as possible. This has always been the goal of the largely White and conservative Federalist Society. While many Republicans had strong ideological differences with Trump, they supported his judicial nominees because he was their path to maintaining Whiteness throughout the country.

So when Justice Ruth Bader Ginsburg died in September 2020, it was no surprise that less than two hours after the announcement of her death, Mitch McConnell declared that he would do everything in his power to ensure that Trump secured her replacement before the end of his term. It made no difference that he and his fellow Republican senators soundly contradicted everything that they said in February 2016 when Obama had the same opportunity after the death of Antonin Scalia.

Justice Ginsburg's woefully inadequate replacement, Amy Coney Barrett, had been a federal judge for all of three years before becoming a Supreme Court Justice. At just forty-eight years old and the former clerk to Justice Antonin Scalia, Barrett officially locked in a conservative majority on the court for at least the next two generations. Not only is Amy Coney Barrett unfit to be a Supreme Court justice, she is also detrimental to the rights of women. Lara Bazelon, a law professor at the University of San Francisco, noted in the *New York Times*:

> Women aren't gym socks, purchased in bulk so that a replacement can be seamlessly substituted into the rotation when one goes missing in the washing machine. The next Supreme Court justice will cast crucial votes that affect women's fundamental rights, including the right to control their own bodies and to gain access to affordable health care for themselves and their families. The fact that President Trump's nominee is a woman matters less if she does not support the causes at the heart of the long, continuing march for gender equality that Justice Ginsburg championed.
>
> Make no mistake: Judge Barrett's confirmation will be the wrecking ball that finally smashes *Roe v. Wade* and undoes the Affordable Care Act. Her crucial vote on these cases and so many others will undo decades of the progress that Justice Ginsburg worked her whole life to achieve.

THE HAUNTING OF *DRED SCOTT* AND *PLESSY V. FERGUSON*

When we analyze the *Dred Scott v. Sandford* case of 1857, Scott sued for the freedom of himself, his wife, and his daughters. He reasoned that because he and his family lived in Illinois for four years, which was declared a free state where slavery was illegal, that they should have the right to live as freed people.

The Civil Rights Act of 1875 was designed to remedy the mass civil rights violations against Blacks in the South during Reconstruction. The bill was supposed to "protect all citizens in their civil and legal rights and provide for equal treatment in public accommodations and public transportation." However, the ruling was repealed in 1883 because President Chester Arthur needed to suppress this law to win during his re-election campaign in the South. The repeal effectively declared that Congress could not outlaw segregation.

Fast-forward to *Plessy v. Ferguson* in 1896, and the Supreme Court in a seven-to-one decision again ruled that racial segregation in public facilities was constitutional as long as they were "separate but equal." The ruling in *Plessy* effectively undid most of the progress that freed Blacks had achieved during Reconstruction. All three of these cases firmly cemented the rule of Jim Crow in the South and another civil rights law would not be passed until 1957.

BROWN V. BOARD OF EDUCATION

Jack Bass's book *Unlikely Heroes* brilliantly articulates the fight that Judges Elbert P. Tuttle from Georgia, John Minor Wisdom from Louisiana, Richard T. Rives from Alabama, and John R.

Brown from Texas took on in the Fifth Circuit Court of Appeals as they interpreted the landmark decision of the U.S. Supreme Court in 1954 that racial segregation in public schools was unconstitutional. After *Brown v. Board of Education*, they boldly interpreted the ruling to make a firm declaration for racial justice and equality under law. Tuttle, Wisdom, and Brown were Republicans when White Democrats still ruled the South. Their input into selected federal judges in the Jim Crow South was crucial for the rulings that would come out of this judicial district for the next two decades.

There were constant battles in Mississippi, Alabama, Louisiana, South Carolina, and Virginia to debunk the validity of *Brown*. The Louisiana legislature, in particular, would pass laws to keep Blacks from integrating the schools. Civil rights lawyers would go to the federal courts to slap them with an injunction stopping the law. The legislature would come back the next day and pass another law, only to again be stopped by the courts with another injunction, and the cycle would repeat. In Louisiana, they even threatened to shut down the entire school system.

After the Supreme Court struck down the separate-but-equal clause in *Brown*, these four judges filled in the gap to define how social, political, and economic institutions would enforce the law. As they interpreted these mandates, the Fifth Circuit Court of Appeals became the legal battleground for the movement. Only a month after Frank Johnson became a federal judge, he and

Richard Rives sat on a three-judge panel to hear the Montgomery bus boycott case in Alabama. Their two-to-one opinion helped to apply *Brown* to a non-school situation, which charted the path for the Fifth Circuit to be a court that set tremendous precedents for the Civil Rights Movement.

While these four judges were revolutionary renegades of their time, they still could not overcome the challenge of Whiteness. There were still conservative southern Dixiecrats who were going to fight for segregation until they died. It didn't matter whether these laws were the right thing to do, Whiteness was always at the top of the agenda. No court would ever be able to fully grant Black Americans the right to be acknowledged as equal citizens.

THE CIVIL RIGHTS BACKLASH

Even while many historians credited President Johnson with the major legislative wins in the 1960s, including the Civil Rights Act of 1964, the Voting Rights Act of 1965, and the Fair Housing Act of 1968, take note that he had to break up these bills into three different pieces of legislation because Congress would not pass his original bill in 1964 that included all three of these provisions.

The Fair Housing Act of 1968 was filibustered for two years and was only broken by Republican Edward Brooke of Massachusetts, the first Black person elected to the Senate since

Reconstruction. Brooke was an ardent supporter of fair housing, but while his arguments were powerful enough to move an all-White senate, the bill never made it out of the House. It continued to be stalled in the House, and it was only the assassination of Dr. Martin Luther King Jr. on April 4, 1968, that led to its passage.

Even with the major breakthrough with the Fair Housing Act of 1968, White Americans still didn't want Black people anywhere near their neighborhoods. After the major civil rights wins in the 1960s, there were now major fights in the 1970s with federal judges ruling on the constitutionality of busing in schools. Many White folks said, "Fine, you can have your schools. But you can't send our kids to another school district just to say that things are equal now."

Because the courts were responsible for enforcing these laws, most White Americans hated the courts during this time; they were being forced into a new era where they couldn't keep their precious resources all to themselves. White folks were beginning to declare that these laws were eroding their civil liberties. Barry Goldwater, the conservative five-term senator from Arizona, then wrote the bible of conservatism that the Republican Party followed for the next forty years, *The Conscience of a Conservative*. You can see how his philosophy keenly shaped Ronald Reagan's run for the presidency in 1976 and his eventual win in 1980. With the addition of *Roe v. Wade*, the Women's Liberation Movement, and other equal rights battles during the 1970s, most

White Americans hated the courts because the laws would no longer allow them to exclude others from their precious vision of the American Dream.

For Black Americans, our only place to redress the evils of racism was on the federal level. Most of the pain inflicted on us came from local and state legislation. Appealing to the larger government for assistance was necessary because local mayors, police departments, and state courts usually ruled against equal rights for people of color.

However, when White America started to catch on, they realized that they had to control the courts to stop all of these federal mandates that were making America an equal playing ground. When Ronald Reagan became president, we saw him appointing and empowering incredibly conservative judges such as Robert Bork and William Rehnquist, both of whom did not believe in civil rights. The court system was even more detrimental to the causes of Black Americans after Justice Rehnquist became Chief Justice under Reagan.

But the same antics the Trump administration pulled in the fall of 2020 were from the playbook that President George H. W. Bush used when he nominated Clarence Thomas to replace Thurgood Marshall. Republicans predicted, correctly, that Democrats would find themselves in a difficult position because, like Justice Marshall, the nominee was Black. But Clarence Thomas was the exact opposite of Marshall in every single way by being outright hostile to civil rights, affirmative action, and most of the claims raised by criminal defendants, who are disproportionately people of color.

Today, with the six-to-three conservative majority in the Supreme Court now firmly in place for at least the next decade, there are key pieces of legislation on the line that could be in jeopardy as America becomes more of a majority minority nation. As I write this book in 2022, there is hope with the Biden-Harris administration controlling the White House and both houses of Congress, but this judicial fight is one that Democrats have to find a way to counter, using the courts the way they were designed to be used, to make this country an equal society for everyone.

CHAPTER EIGHT

REDEFINING THE AMERICAN VOTING BOOTH

"We are tired of being beaten by policemen. We're tired of seeing our people locked up in jail over and over again. And then you holler, 'Be patient.' How long can we be patient? We want our freedom and we want it now."

—Future Representative John Lewis, speaking at the March on Washington for Jobs and Freedom in 1963

There's a reason why some of the bloodiest and deadliest battles of the Civil Rights Movement were over voting rights. In this country in particular, we have defined citizenship by the ability to vote. If you are not able to vote, you are not a full citizen. That's why we punish people with taking away their right to vote. John Lewis understood that voting is power, voting determines who sits on juries, voting determines what resources a community has both at the local and federal level, and whether we will enforce civil rights law or not.

John Lewis had always led the way in fighting injustice. He was one of the central figures who led protestors across the Edmund Pettus Bridge in Selma. The event was later dubbed "Bloody Sunday" after rampant violence broke out and many protestors were hospitalized. Lewis became widely known for making what has been called necessary trouble, fighting for his ideals and pushing for necessary change such as the Voting Rights Act of 1965. He brought that attitude to the U.S. House of Representatives in 1986, when he was elected to represent Georgia's fifth district. He was often called the "Conscience of Congress" because of his unwavering moral code. Despite his activism leading up to and through his seventeen terms in Congress, by the time of his death in 2020 he witnessed a movement that looked very much like the movement he was involved with in the 1960s.

So here we are in 2022, fifty-four years after Dr. King's assassination. As we see the civil rights lions pass away, we're still fighting for the very same things because we have yet to be a nation that has provided Black folks to be full American citizens. If we truly want to honor the legacy of champions such as John Lewis, we would be more serious about mobilizing, organizing, and voting to kick out the very people in Congress, in state capitals, and in county commissions courts who are denying people their rights as Americans.

The 2020 election was expected to be the first election where less than 70 percent of the electorate were White voters. But Trump pushed the buttons of White voters and their White Fear directly translated to a big turnout at the polls, where 72 to 74 percent of all voters were White.

We can clearly see how these fears played out with major voter suppression efforts during the 2016 general election and voter irregularities during the 2018 gubernatorial races in Florida and Georgia.

In her 2018 gubernatorial race, Stacey Abrams ran a bold progressive campaign to energize new voters in a brand-new way. Her campaign wasn't about flipping the tried-and-true Reagan voters back to their pre-1980s Democratic leanings. She was focused on bringing out an electorate who had been denied and suppressed for generations. It speaks to the testament of her character that she didn't just stop when she lost the gubernatorial race. She saw the bigger picture of being able to affect a historic presidential race for the first time in a generation.

Black voters defied the odds and came out in record-breaking numbers. Black people, particularly Black women, have always voted at very high rates. Black women are voting at the highest rates of all groups right now. Black people have had the right to vote since the Fifteenth Amendment in 1870. What has not been so clear is our ability to exercise that right. In 2018 there was also incredible mobilization of the state's Latino voters (at 12 percent), women voters (at 52 percent), and LGBTQIA and first-time college voters. The Republican Party now has to contend with the fact that Georgia flipped for a Democratic presidential nominee for the first time in twenty-eight years and gained two Democratic Senate seats and a congressional seat. But these votes were drowned out by draconian voter suppression laws, from using outdated die-bolt machines that have been phased out in most of the country to gerrymandering the map every election cycle. There was enough support to get 200,000 purged voters back on the rolls. There was enough grassroots support to turn out 90,000 voters who never voted before.

We clearly saw how the valiant work of Stacey Abrams and other grassroots organizations throughout the battleground states of Michigan, Wisconsin, and Arizona delivered a solid blue win for the Biden–Harris campaign just a few years later.

As early as August 2020, we saw all of the changes that were happening in Georgia to accommodate voters in light of COVID-19. There were measures to encourage early in-person voting and mail-in ballots. Turnout for early voting in the general election was overwhelmingly popular and positive as some voters in DeKalb and Fulton Counties reported waiting in line for as long as eleven hours.

But on Saturday, November 6, 2020, for the first time in twenty-eight years, a Democratic candidate won the state of Georgia by 12,000 votes. The voters of Georgia did it again on January 5, 2021, as they decisively added Raphael Warnock and Jon Ossoff as the newest Democratic senators from the state, with Warnock becoming the first Black senator for Georgia. On the backside of this runoff election in Georgia, we saw that Kelly Loeffler and David Perdue were clearly intimidated by the power of Warnock and Ossoff turning out the Black vote in voluminous numbers. And they had every right to be scared as they're both now tossed to the sidelines and are nothing more than yesterday's headlines.

What Georgia accomplished in 2020 is akin to what North Carolina did to usher Obama into the White House in 2008. Several grassroots organizations registered new voters and successfully implemented measures to encourage early voter registration and early in-person voting for Black voters and college students who were voting for the first time. The result was that Obama won North Carolina by 14,100 votes.

However, this victory was very short lived as Republican representatives in North Carolina then gained majority control of the state legislature and put significant voter suppression laws in place that required voter IDs and cut back on early voting options. It would take another ten years before the 2008 grassroots efforts could regain any of the ground that they had lost.

But as usual with Black success at the voting booth, White Fear soon followed with Donald Trump's vicious and racist attacks on Black voters in Detroit, Philadelphia, Milwaukee, and Atlanta. His followers were quickly outraged that their White supremacist "god" could be voted out of office. The 2020 presidential election was contested right up to Inauguration Day. There are still Republican members of Congress who are debating those results today.

In 2021 with the White House, Senate, and House clearly secured for the Democrats for two years, it was no surprise that Governor Kemp in Georgia, Governor Abbott in Texas, and Governor DeSantis in Florida immediately implemented some of the most drastic voter suppression laws in a generation. These severe measures don't surprise most Black Americans, but what White America needs to understand is that their silence on these measures means that they are complicit. They have to understand what Black people have always understood: You cannot give an inch to racists, especially at the voting booth.

THE IMPACT OF *SHELBY COUNTY V. HOLDER*

Why were states like North Carolina, Florida, and Georgia able to do all of this? The *Shelby County v. Holder* ruling of 2013 essentially gutted Section 4B of the Voting Rights Act of 1965, which provided a formula for the federal government to use in identifying jurisdictions with problematic histories of racial discrimination.

During the 2013 ruling, Chief Justice John Roberts asserted that the Voting Rights Act did its job of ensuring equal rights for Black people to vote because they overwhelmingly elected Barack Obama to office. His faulty logic was that the Voting Rights Act was no longer needed because Black people were consistently exercising their right to vote, a rationale that ignored that the reason Black people were able to vote in record numbers in the first place was because of the Voting Rights Act. The Supreme Court asserted that Section 4 was unconstitutional because it applied only to states with rampant voter discrimination policies during the 1950s and 1960s. The court ruled that the formula used for the section was outdated and Congress had the right to update it.

The Voting Rights Act of 1965 was a bipartisan bill that could be gutted and repealed at any time. The Republican Party is keenly aware that to win elections they must shrink the electorate. Therefore, when *Shelby County v. Holder* was upheld in the Supreme Court, that was a huge win for the GOP and state GOP legislatures in particular. To maintain Whiteness, the Republican Party knows that they have to create barriers to keep people from voting.

Since *Shelby County v. Holder*, Republicans have used state legislatures for political gerrymandering to redraw district and county lines. We have seen the sharp uptick in voter ID laws, reverse limits on early voting, and the purging of voter rolls in many states with Republican-led state legislatures, such as

Tennessee, South Carolina, North Carolina, Alabama, Florida, Mississippi, Arkansas, and Louisiana. It's no surprise that these are southern states with large Black populations. This is how the GOP has been able to control voting. They do not want to see expanded voting rights.

Republicans in these states used the same basic method. They closed polling locations, a lot of them in Black areas. They made it harder by imposing voter ID laws. All of a sudden, they created a tsunami of hurdles that people had to jump over, frustrating Black voters. And the Republicans didn't just target Black people; they also went after White folks because they saw that there were too many young White people voting Democrat. So, what did they do? They started removing early voting locations from college campuses. They removed convenient voting locations and moved them to far-out places with small parking lots to create long lines and lots of frustration.

So, how in the world did the Voting Rights Act get gutted under the administration of the first Black president? It was because of the conservative majority in the Supreme Court. The courts on the state level then applied the ruling, which gave state legislatures the right to begin enforcing voter suppression laws with the most drastic measures. The Republicans had controlled both houses of Congress, so it was relatively easy to begin their plot to control the courts and then begin suppressing the Black vote even further.

Beyond Section 4 of the Voting Rights Act, Section 2 prohibits voting practices or procedures that discriminate on the basis of race, color, or membership in a large minority group. This part of the Voting Rights Act was heard before the Supreme Court in August 2021 and of course they ruled in favor of Arizona, saying their charges were not discriminatory. This conservative Supreme Court is even closer to fulfilling the dream of Clarence Thomas: a complete wipeout of the 1965 Voting Rights Act.

Now with the Supreme Court consisting of a conservative majority, there are relevant fears that voting rights for Black, Latino, and Asian populations will revert back to square one and onerous voting restrictions will be enacted at the state level. Democrats are desperate to fix this with new federal voting laws, but have so far been stymied by Senators Kyrsten Sinema and Joe Manchin, who reject the idea of getting rid of the filibuster in order to pass them.

Way before *Shelby County v. Holder*, the Fifteenth Amendment guaranteed African American men the right to vote in 1870, and we have to consider the role that laws at the federal level have played in empowering African Americans. Black people have been adversely impacted by federal, state, and county laws. But our redress has always been taken care of by the federal government, especially when it comes to voting. The Fifteenth Amendment was huge because it led to an explosion of Black people being elected to state and federal legislatures all across the South. African Americans were well represented in the state legislatures in South Carolina, North Carolina, and Mississippi during the early days of Reconstruction.

But the reality is that the Fifteenth Amendment *had* to be passed because prior to Reconstruction, land-owning Black men had already been voting in sizable numbers. Then states began withdrawing voting rights for freed Black men. Virginia was the first state to revoke these rights in the 1850s, and soon other states followed suit. So it's not that Black people first got the right to vote with the Fifteenth Amendment. The Fifteenth Amendment restored our right to vote and to be seen as actual Americans.

Having the right to vote meant that Black people would have the full citizenship rights of all Americans. Essentially White Southerners said, "Well, we're not going to see you all as citizens, so we have to pass a law that says you all get the right to vote." Then after Reconstruction, they put in all these different barriers in place, to again keep Black Americans from voting.

Beyond the implications for Black voters, White Fear has also had detrimental effects on Latino, Asian, and Native American voters. Similar to Black Americans, White America likes to write Latino voters off as infrequent voters and are thus blindsided when they show up at the polls in forceful numbers. From a power-building standpoint, the reality is that politics is a game of addition, of building bridges and alliances. Although there may be profound differences among minority groups, our adversaries see us all as the same: a threat. Latinos are a multinational, multiracial, and multiethnic group that has a history of working together for justice as well.

The emergence of Asian American voters in Georgia and Michigan was also a bright spot during the 2020 election. Asian Americans are the fastest-growing segment of eligible new voters out of the major racial and ethnic groups in the country. Nationally, voter participation among Asian Americans has historically been low: In 2016, they had the second-lowest turnout after Hispanics of all major groups. Now, Asian immigrants have reached a critical mass and their children, now entering their thirties and forties and many of them educated in the United States, are pushing for more representation.

Native American voters were also a formidable voting bloc in metropolitan areas like Phoenix and Tucson, Arizona. While these areas voted overwhelmingly Democratic, White voters should not underestimate the value of indigenous voters becoming a more vital engine in future elections.

REDISTRICTING AND GERRYMANDERING HAS CONSEQUENCES

Redistricting in places like Texas, Georgia, and Florida will test whether minority population gains will translate into political clout. Ninety-five percent of the population growth in Texas has been a result of non-Whites. The word is that there are more Democrats moving to Texas and that the population will change with the growth of the Latino community and the growing power of Blacks. But even with these gains, there are still Republicans who are working very hard to disenfranchise voters of color in Texas.

In Mississippi, after the passage of the Civil Rights Act of 1964, right before the passage of the Voting Rights Act of 1965, only 6.9 percent of Blacks were registered to vote. After the Voting Rights Act passed, that number went up to 60 percent in 1966. And then, when Blacks went out to vote, there was a counter-mobilization by Whites to suppress the Black vote. If you fast-forward to today, you see the exact same thing happening in terms of the suppression of voting.

I'm still registered to vote in Texas, and I can tell you there is no greater threat to democracy in the United States than the Republican Party in Texas. Listening to the gutless leadership of Governor Greg Abbott and Lieutenant Governor Dan Patrick shows how sick and demented these people are. There was a news conference during which Patrick said, "How dare you question his integrity and that of eighteen Republicans in the United States Senate?"

But we actually can because it is all based on a lie.

Here's what's going on in Texas: Democrats have been highly successful in Harris County (Houston), Dallas County (Dallas), and Bexar County (San Antonio), the larger counties in Texas. They have decimated the Republican Party in the suburbs. The Democrats were a few seats away from taking control of the Texas House in the 2020 election. Republicans realize the Latino population is driving an increase in congressional seats. They want to maintain power as much as they can, frankly, for their largely White base. What they have been doing is protecting their incumbents, and that's why they are scrambling to suppress voting.

The state senate has passed a bill limiting extended early voting hours, prohibiting drive-through voting, banning local election officials from proactively sending vote-by-mail applications, and allowing poll watchers to videotape voters receiving assistance in filling out their ballots, essentially allowing poll watchers to intimidate voters.

All of this is based off of dear leader Donald's election lie, a delusional and racist fantasy that he and the GOP made up as an excuse for losing the presidency, the Senate, the House, and scores of local legislative seats across the country.

This isn't about protecting voting; this is the actual fraud. It's a desperate power grab aimed at preventing the opposition from voting.

Donald Trump put 25 percent of the federal judiciary on the bench, which means a lot more right-wing judges who don't care about voting rights. This is why voting matters: Even if you don't care about the presidential race, you should care that federal judges who do not care about racial gerrymandering are gaining power.

THE CALL FOR BLACK REPUBLICANS

What's even more egregious are the gutless black Republicans who know what they're doing, which is embarrassing the elders, embarrassing the ancestors, and they know what the Republican party is doing, which is a direct assault on Black and Latino voters.

Conservatives in the Black community can, of course, enter the arena and compete in the field of ideas. What angers me about Black Republicans such as Senator Tim Scott and Congressmen Burgess Owens and Byron Donald is their lack of courage to stand up to their party. I wish they would be like the late Republican Senator Edward Brooke, the first African American elected to the Senate since Reconstruction, who stood up to Southern Democrats and moderate Republicans and stopped the filibuster of the Fair Housing Act in 1968. Senator Brooke was also the senator who kept reintroducing bills to get Martin Luther King Jr. recognized with a federal holiday (the late Michigan Democratic Representative John Conyers pushed it in the House).

There is still an opportunity for Black Republicans to do the right thing, to come out against what their party is doing. Stand up and call out your party by saying, "This is not right."

How do we keep up the momentum of the 2020 election without falling prey to the frustration of long lines, voter ID restrictions, and misinformation about election policy? We have to keep up this same enthusiasm for every election season, and not just the general elections. We have to show this same enthusiasm for midterm elections and ensure that the weight of these elections doesn't fall just on one group to show up and make the difference at the polls.

White Fear can be perpetuated only when Black voters become complacent and rely on the same folks to carry us across the finish line. There are no Black saviors coming to rescue us from this American nightmare. Extinguishing White Fear means that every person of color has to show up and do their part to ensure that we never face another White House administration where our needs are soundly dismissed and disregarded by a Racist in Chief.

The 2020 election gave us the playbook to see what is possible when we come together to defeat White Fear. And even though 75 million Americans voted to keep White Fear in place, we now know what kind of America we can create when possibility trumps White Fear.

Vertner Woodson Tandy, one of my Alpha Phi Alpha fraternity brothers, said it best back in 1937: "We will fight until hell freezes over—and then we will fight on the ice." There is no greater issue for Black folks than the fundamental right to vote—and that will never change.

WHEN WHITE FEAR COMES KNOCKING AT THE DOOR

In this final section of *White Fear*, I will lay out how the persistent fears of White America have affected the everyday lives of people of color from their ability to buy homes and build equity to their ability to gain access to an equal education, and the continued disproportionate effects of policing on Black bodies.

CHAPTER NINE

THE FIGHT TO EDUCATE BLACK MINDS

Historical Black colleges and universities have had a significant influence on American history and culture, graduating leaders across all fields for more than 150 years. HBCUs have also been instrumental in leading movements and change in the African American community. The cases that set the precedent for *Brown v. Board of Education* started at Howard University; the Woolworth sit-ins began at North Carolina A&T; and HBCU students all across the South were pivotal agents for change with the Freedom Riders, the Student Nonviolent Coordinating Committee (SNCC), and voter registration drives throughout the Civil Rights Movement. For many Black students, attending an HBCU is one of the rare opportunities in their academic career where they are in the majority and where they have the intellectual freedom to just be without the looming threat of Whiteness.

During the 2018-19 academic year, Dillard University in New Orleans graduated fourteen African Americans majoring in physics. Harvard produced exactly one. Harvard's got all the money in the world. The absolute smartest students, the most brilliant professors. Are they actually producing? Among the hundreds of African American students at Harvard, how many are getting the resources and support to complete their undergraduate degrees? They're not graduating enough of those students. Schools like Dillard, Howard, and Xavier are, and yet we're not giving these schools credit where credit is due.

HBCUs have also been one of the biggest engines for African Americans to move into the middle class. There are thousands of Black middle-class families who have had multiple generations attend HBCUs, which creates new futures and new avenues for growth that many of us were not able to obtain without an education. Education still is the most vital issue facing Black people because it's tied to income equality. If we are getting educated, we are on a much better path to being empowered. If you don't have an education, you are screwed in America. And if you don't have an education and you're Black? Forget about it.

I know that people are still needlessly debating the need for HBCUs in the twenty-first century, but the case remains very clear why these institutions are incredibly vital for Black students. When it comes to our colleges, HBCUs were the only options for Black Americans after Reconstruction. The challenge that we are still fighting is that HBCUs have been underfunded for decades, with billions of dollars in state funding that should have gone to those schools diverted by lawmakers for other purposes. Many HBCU presidents and school leaders have been pushing for decades to get the money that these institutions are rightfully owed. College presidents and local lawmakers in Tennessee and Maryland have spent years poring over state budgets to calculate those funding gaps and to justify how that funding will benefit Black students.

In 2021, Maryland HBCUs were finally awarded $577 million to be distributed over ten years, but only after a thirteen-year legal battle with the state. Governor Larry Hogan reluctantly signed the bill after the Democratic legislature defied his veto. In the summer of 2021, Khristopher Brooks reported the following for CBS News:

> In a federal lawsuit for Maryland HBCUs, the schools argued that they were being purposely underfunded compared with mostly White colleges in the state. Dozens of HBCUs have operated for years without receiving the full amount of dollars they were entitled to under the law. One study from the Association of Public and Land-grant Universities found that, between 2010 and 2012, more than half the nation's HBCUs failed to get their full funding.

Most HBCUs receive significantly less state and federal funding and research development than their White counterparts.

Each year, Congress allots millions for public HBCUs and states are supposed to match the federal dollars each school receives. Brooks further reported that:

> HBCU presidents and education experts said that match rarely happens in practice, pointing to a general refusal by state lawmakers over many years to match the federal investment. In Tennessee, state budget officials uncovered that Tennessee State University has been underfunded by roughly $544 million dating back to 1950. The state arrived at that figure after a committee of lawmakers in 2020 started looking into underfunding at the school.

In Mississippi in the late 1990s, there was a lawsuit similar to the Maryland and Tennessee cases where Mississippi HBCUs won a settlement for approximately $516 million. If you translate that into today's value, that figure is close to $800 million. While I'm sure Maryland HBCUs in particular are grateful for the $577 million they were finally awarded in 2021, in reality that number should be closer to $1 billion to account for inflation after a nearly two-decade battle to get the money they deserve.

———————

Meanwhile, as HBCUs continue fighting tooth and nail to get adequate and equal funding, for Black students who want to attend predominantly White institutions, White Fear continues to thwart Black progress with the never-ending battles over affirmative action in education. Affirmative action has always been a huge issue in America. Black folks have been left out of predominantly White universities for quite some time. But one of the things that changed was universities being forced with affirmative action to diversify and to include more students of color.

In 2012, there was a White woman, Abigail Fisher, who sued the University of Texas because she and her lawyers claimed that she was denied admission because of the increase in admissions for Black and Latino students. She was recruited by Edward Blum, who has orchestrated several efforts to attack civil rights. He initially went after voting rights in the 1960s and 1970s, and for the past decade he has set his sights on tearing down affirmative action efforts at Ivy League and elite colleges and universities. Fisher's case went all the way to the Supreme Court, where she lost, because it was discovered that these Black and Brown students were indeed more than qualified to attend *and* that many of the White students who were admitted were accepted due to legacy admissions. On average, there are twice as many White students getting into these schools despite having lower qualifications and connections than there are Black and Brown students getting in with even a little bit of help from affirmative action.

Keep in mind that these kids like Abigail Fisher who went to a "more rigorous school" and took more AP classes didn't earn that education. They were born into a family that could afford it. How in the world is somebody entitled to that education? White students are not more entitled to a fair education than someone else simply because that other person was born in a rural or urban area.

When you take a step back and dig into this further, many students of color are already at a disadvantage when it comes to preparation for the SATs and other standardized testing. On average, we know that the SAT and other standardized test scores are the biggest single correlation with your zip code and the quality of the school that you attended from kindergarten through grade twelve. We have such a profoundly unequal K-12 system that, by definition, you are going to have a disproportionate number of White folks who are going to test better because they have better access to SAT preparation and tutoring. You are going to have a disproportionate number of Black and Brown folks who test lower irrespective of their real potential.

Before Blum's failed attempt to challenge affirmative action with Abigail Fisher, there was the 1996 *Hopwood* case in Texas in which the U.S. Court of Appeals for the Fifth Circuit held that the University of Texas School of Law could not use race as a factor in determining which applicants could be admitted.

This case rose to prominence because White legislators were receiving complaints from White parents that rural White kids were not getting into the University of Texas, Texas A&M, Texas

Tech, North Texas, and all the other major state universities. The minority legislators met with the rural White legislators and said, "Okay, we're going to admit the top 10 percent." That is, if you finish in the top 10 percent of your graduating class, you would be automatically admitted to any state university in Texas. Guess what happened? Those rich White parents said, "Well, wait a minute. My child goes to a much more rigorous school. And it's unfair for that poor White kid, Black kid, or Latino kid to get into the University of Texas and mine doesn't, when my child takes mostly AP honors classes."

So, what did they do? The University of Texas had them slash the number of people who were admitted under the top 10 percent by saying, "We don't have enough room to be able to pick more minority students." So even when you have a nonrace-based model, you still have rich or well-to-do White parents who still say, "No, we ain't down with this because they're getting the hookup and we are not."

When Ed Blum's case with Abigail Fisher failed, he doubled down by creating a group called the Students for Fair Admissions. The group believes that the elite Ivy League schools are somehow hurting White kids by what conservative critics call reverse discrimination. This group is looking for Asian American students who will be a wedge group to help Blum mount claims against affirmative action efforts at colleges and universities. The Students for Fair Admissions claims that Asian

Americans are being rejected for less-qualified African American and Latino students. This claim is absolutely outrageous because African Americans and Latinos are more underrepresented at elite major colleges and universities today than they were thirty-five years ago.

Harvard's class of 2021 was 50.9 percent minority groups: 22.2 percent Asian, 14.6 percent African American, 11.6 percent Latino, 2.5 percent Native American or Pacific Islander. Asian American students actually benefited the most from affirmative action programs at these elite schools, so it was ridiculous for this group to want to tear down the affirmative action program because they claimed more Asian American students would be admitted into Harvard and other elite institutions without it.

At the time of the investigation, Harvard released this statement to *Newsweek*:

> To become leaders in our diverse society, students must have the ability to work with people from different backgrounds, life experiences, and perspectives. Harvard remains committed to enrolling diverse classes of students. Harvard's admissions process considers each applicant as a whole person, and we review many factors consistent with the legal standards established by the U.S. Supreme Court.

Using Asian American students as a scapegoat for affirmative action actually ends up hurting everyone except for very elite White students. So, when you bring it back around to how students are actually admitted to schools, it's amazing how the same people who love complaining about affirmative action don't want anyone to touch legacy admissions. White legacy students today are benefiting from past segregation; they're getting a leg up because African Americans and Latino students can't use this same system, because our parents and grandparents couldn't have gone to those schools.

In 2004 at the UNITY: Journalists of Color Convention in Washington, DC, four journalists of color, which included Native American, Latino, Asian, and African American journalists, got a chance to ask President George W. Bush a series of questions. The National Association of Black Journalists (NABJ) chose me to represent our organization. At this time, the Michigan affirmative action case was going before the United States Supreme Court. I chose to ask former President Bush about his views on quotas and affirmative action. Here's a bit of our conversation:

ROLAND MARTIN: The president of Texas A&M, Robert Gates, said that he would not use race in admissions. And then he later said, he would continue to use legacy. If you say it's a matter of merit and not race, shouldn't colleges also get rid of legacy? And because that's not based upon merit, that's based upon if my daddy or my granddaddy went to my college.

GEORGE W. BUSH: Well, in my case, I had to knock on a lot of doors to follow the old man's footsteps. If what you're saying is, is there are going to be special treatment for people? And there was, we're going to have a special exception for certain people and a system that's supposed to be fair? I agree. I don't think there ought to be.

ROLAND MARTIN: So, the colleges should get rid of legacy?

GEORGE W. BUSH: Well, I think so. I think it ought to be based upon merit. And I think it also be based upon . . . And I think colleges need to work hard for diversity. No, don't get me wrong. Or, now, get me wrong. You said against affirmative actions, what you said. You put words in my mouth.

ROLAND MARTIN: So, you support affirmative action but not quotas?

GEORGE W. BUSH: I support colleges affirmatively taking action to get more minorities in their school.

ROLAND MARTIN: That's a long headline, Mr. President.

GEORGE W. BUSH: I support diversity. I don't support quotas. I think quotas are wrong. I think quotas are wrong for people. And so do a lot of people.

ROLAND MARTIN: But just to be clear, you believe that colleges should not use legacy?

GEORGE W. BUSH: I think colleges ought to use merit in order for people to get in. And I think they ought to use a merit system like the one I put out.

After that questioning of President Bush, the *New York Times* ran a story the next day, and there were tons of phone calls to Yale, Harvard, and so on, from concerned folks there saying, "Oh my goodness, are you all going to get rid of legacy?"

If you're a student at Yale or Harvard or Columbia, chances are you came from a wealthy background. You went to the highest quality high school. Your parents can provide for your every need. When you graduate, you're going to get a fantastic job. You have everything going for you. Why can't you then stand up and say, "All right. In this one respect, my school has benefited from this crazy biased ranking system. Let's all get together and say this is one small part of our privilege that we can surrender." I am waiting for the student activists at the big Ivy League schools to stand up and say that.

CHAPTER TEN

FIGHTING THE BLUE WALL

An October 2021 study from the *Lancet* showed that killings by police in this country are routinely undercounted. More than 55 percent of deaths related to police violence were assigned to other causes, which accounts for a total of about 17,000 police killings that are mislabeled. The study also shows police mislabeled the killings of Black men at higher rates than for any other race. The *Lancet* report also points out that accountability is also lacking, with only 1 percent of officers involved in killings charged with a crime. This data comes as Republicans and Democrats in Congress still have not reached an agreement on police reform. In October 2021, Senator Cory Booker said,

> We should be in a nation that if an officer uses physical force, that data should be collected. We live in a country where

both Senator Scott and I have had personal experiences with wrongfully stopped, being stopped by police, guns drawn on us, accused of things that we didn't do. If there's no transparency into those actions, we can't deal with it.

As much as Republicans rally about law and order, they are always very quiet when it comes to police reforms and challenging police unions. Pro-lifers are very quiet. White, conservative Evangelicals are quiet. This is why George Floyd's family is not happy with Senator Tim Scott, Senator Lindsey Graham, and other Republicans for not making the George Floyd Justice in Policing Act real. Police violence against Black people has been a fundamental problem we've seen in this country for far too long. It's time for Republicans to step up, get involved, and hold police officers accountable for their actions.

In September 2021, Attorney General Merrick Garland reversed the Trump administration's limits on consent decrees. Under the last administration, the Department of Justice (DOJ) used these decrees to require police departments that were accused of misconduct to reform. This policy reversal comes after a series of murders involving police, particularly the death of George Floyd in Minneapolis in May 2020. While Garland's reversal of this act is what should have been done in the first place, one of the problems the DOJ faces with these investigations is the fact that their resources are finite. If you've got a hundred police departments across the country that have significant issues, the DOJ doesn't have the resources to go in and reform each of these departments. The DOJ provides technical grants, which come with funding, to help the police department transform itself. However, this needs to be billed as a productive process that works well for everyone, citizens and police alike. The effort by the prior presidential administration to posture it as something that was anti-police is just wrong.

THE DEPARTMENT OF JUSTICE IS WORTHLESS WITHOUT LOCAL ENFORCEMENT

What we have to realize is that changes to policing aren't going to happen in Washington, DC. Change has to happen in local law enforcement agencies. Since the Derek Chauvin trial in the spring of 2021, Attorney General Merrick Garland announced that the DOJ is going to investigate police practices in Minneapolis. They announced they're going to do the same thing in Louisville, Kentucky. The mayor of Columbus, Ohio, where forty people have been killed by police since 2013, is calling on the DOJ to come in as well.

Now, the problem is that the Department of Justice can come in, but if the local police department does not put into practice what is recommended, they fail. In Chicago, the DOJ came in and made recommendations, and the Chicago police department did not put into practice what they recommended, so they still have problems. Local officials must be willing to stand up to police unions, police departments, and to the public, and say, "We are not going to kowtow to the old school notion of whatever the police want, they get." We need leadership. We've got to put people in charge, including DAs, judges, city managers, city mayors, city council members, who are going to be far more aggressive when it comes to these problematic police departments. This is the only way we can move toward true reform.

Before the killings of George Floyd and Breonna Taylor galvanized the nation, you had the modern lynching of Ahmaud Arbery in Georgia in February 2020. A grand jury charged three defendants in Arbery's death with federal hate crimes and kidnapping charges in November 2021, and in February 2022 they were found guilty. While the defendants in the Arbery case were not law enforcement officers, they did have relationships with prosecutors in their county, which critics cast as central to why the defendants were not charged for months. Reforming police departments is one thing, but it has to go hand in hand with reform in the legal system itself.

THE IMPORTANCE OF DAs

The reality is that more than 80 percent of our district attorneys are White, conservative men. As of this writing, there are outliers such as Marilyn Mosby in Baltimore and Kim Foxx in Chicago, Aramis Ayala in Florida, and White progressives such as Larry Krasner in Philadelphia. When it comes to the outcome of a trial, many people now realize that the DA is just as important as the jury.

When people are running for office in this country, they revere police officers, firefighters, the first responders. If you are running for mayor or district attorney, one of the most coveted endorsements is from those particular unions; politicians understand that power. These powerful unions have ensured that certain laws don't get passed. Progressive activists now understand the value of progressive district attorneys who are not aligned with the police officers.

In the case of Ahmaud Arbery, three different DAs were not moving the case forward. It wasn't until a video of the murder was released that the pressure was put on the Georgia Bureau of Investigation. They stepped in and charges were filed. The public has to understand that voter suppression has a direct impact on who becomes our DAs, since they are elected. If you want law enforcement reform, criminal justice reform, voter suppression must end because that impacts who gets elected. All of these things are interrelated. To have full police reform, we must have top-to-bottom reform, from the president, U.S. Senate, members of Congress, governors, state reps, state senators, DAs, judges— the entire system.

FIGHTING THE BLUE WALL

The greatest "don't snitch" policy in America is in police departments. They don't want to talk. They don't want to turn each other in. They don't want to come out from behind the veil of secrecy—and that's the problem. One reason Black Lives Matter has been so successful is because they have forced the most rigorous discussion of police brutality and accountability in the history of America.

Everybody wants to focus on Congress or on the White House, but the real substantive changes in police departments can happen only when mayors, city councils, and the county commissioners do their jobs. In 2021, Maryland legislators got rid of the police officers' bill of rights in an effort to enact reform. Republican Governor Larry Hogan vetoed it, but they overrode his veto. Local officials are the ones who can greatly impact their police department.

True reform means understanding we need strong local elected officials. They have to have the guts to stand up to police unions and to stand up and fight for citizens. They can't just say, "Oh, DOJ, can y'all come in and save our butts?" We need the courage to make the changes on the local level. We saw the benefits of local pressure in April 2021 when a sheriff's deputy shot and killed a Black man in Elizabeth City, North Carolina, while executing a search warrant and an arrest warrant on drug charges. The local county sheriff did not immediately come forward with the body camera footage or provide any pertinent details from the evening of the shooting for hours, even though residents demanded answers. The city council called an emergency meeting and several Black members shared their frustrations surrounding the shooting.

In this situation, there were two different things going on—the state of emergency and the lack of leadership. African Americans were the majority on the city council, and they declared a state of emergency, which was a concern to some folks. School was made virtual the entire week, but the reality was that the protests were peaceful. The fundamental problem in Elizabeth City—in this county—was that nobody knew who was in charge of the investigation. Who was leading it? The district attorney, Andrew Womble, was "unavailable for five days" when the shooting took place, according to Reverend Anthony Spearman, who is in charge of the local NAACP state conference.

Unlike in Minnesota and other states, the state attorney general cannot take over the case; the DA has to recuse himself, but this DA has chosen not to do so. With all these dynamics at play, the people there rightly voiced that they need to have real transparency to know who's leading the investigation and who's in control of the evidence.

If we want more police reform in this country, it's going to take President Biden being just as concerned and aggressive as he was about his infrastructure bill. In fact, he has to be more aggressive. President Biden has got to do more to put more pressure on the senators and say, "You are not going to let another year go by without the George Floyd Justice in Policing Act being passed." Pressure has to be applied to both sides. As citizens we've got to be in their faces, protesting, showing up at town halls. Wherever senators go, they have to hear, "Y'all got to move on this act." It's going to take people out there putting pressure on Senators Tim Scott, Lindsey Graham, and Mitch McConnell to do more.

I believe the families of George Floyd, Breonna Taylor, Eric Garner, and the many others unjustifiably killed by police should organize a day on Capitol Hill. March up those steps and say, "McConnell, Graham, Scott. We want you at the table. We want Booker and Durbin, as well as Schumer, at the table. We want you to sit in front of us and look us in the eye and tell us why this bill is not real." It's going to take public pressure for America to see the reform it needs.

THE NEW AMERICAN WORLD ORDER

The year 2043—the year when America will become a majority minority country—now forces America to have a different worldview and to accept that we are truly moving toward being a multicultural America. White America always had the majority and were successful in fighting, stalling, preventing, short-circuiting, and subverting the advancements of people of color. Now the numbers are no longer in White America's favor. The numbers are actually now being reversed. White childbirth is the lowest it's ever been; the annual White death rate now exceeds the annual White birth rate.

The march toward 2043 leads to a massive redefining of what America looks like. Now we need major investment in education and housing. Now White America has to figure out how in the hell does it operate in a world it doesn't completely control?

Inching closer to 2043 forces a dramatic and massive readjustment, realignment, and redefinition of what it actually means to be American, and it impacts everything. For example, many Americans have looked at majority Black and Brown nations as third-world countries. However, some of the fastest-growing economies are African nations. It would be beneficial to look at Africa as an economic investment instead of a liability. No longer being a White majority nation forces us also to see nations in South America and the Caribbean outside of the lens of colonialism.

The year 2043 forces a completely different assessment of American values, and this is going to continue to be a struggle for White Americans because they have been raised to think that God's favor has been on America. They believe that America is the greatest country in the world and that we can do no wrong. They've never had to consider that third stanza in "The Star-Spangled Banner." They never had to think about how in some parts of the world when others see the American flag, they see domination and colonization. They never had to factor in how racism in America is viewed abroad and couldn't handle it when people around the world aligned with Angela Davis when she was on trial in 1971. They don't understand how the deaths of Ahmaud Arbery and George Floyd led to massive protests all across the world.

America has always said, "We are the shining light on a hill," but America never wanted to shine that light on itself. But 2043 changes all of that.

We have to prepare the next generation for the changing demographics. Two-thirds of the world's countries are already a majority of people of color and—sooner than we know it—America will be just like the rest of the world. And the prevalence of White Fear will cause the political and economic landscape of America to get a whole lot worse before it gets any better.

THE REALITY OF A 2024 TRUMP CAMPAIGN

When your house is built on a racial foundation, Donald Trump is what you are going to get. Remember how he rose to political prominence?

It was his attacks on the birth certificate of President Barack Obama.

It was his attacks on Mexican Americans.

It was his attacks on Colin Kaepernick and other NFL players.

He knows how to press the buttons of White Fear in America. Donald Trump pushed every racial, sexist, classist, and xenophobic button you could push in this country—and he was *still* elected.

We've got to confront the reality that this man will run again for president in 2024. Donald Trump was a thug in chief. He and his administration were engaged in absolute illegal activity; at some point we have to be willing to say this cannot happen again. We cannot allow these thugs to be in power again. This is not about America or democracy. Republicans are choosing power, even over party. God forbid that thug somehow gets the nomination and comes close to being back in the oval office. If you think the crap that he did for four years was crazy, just watch what this man will try to do with his second term. America is in danger, and this danger is real.

One of the things I'm most worried about is the fact that we don't have guardrails to prevent this from happening. The curtailing of Trump's manipulation depended on good people with integrity who refused to take part. We should all be frightened. It's easy to discount events when you're living through them, so we need to be very focused on what's happening now. Illegally trying to get state legislatures to throw the election to Trump, which Trump and his cronies tried to do after the 2020 election, is now acceptable in a number of states.

At the end of the Civil War there were people who came forward and surrendered, who acknowledged that they had been wrong. Trump has never done that. Trump is dedicated to moving forward. He will do it again.

THE NEXT AGENDA FOR BLACK AMERICA

As people of color moving toward 2043, we have to have a very clear, defined strategy. First and foremost, we have to use this period to completely challenge every system, from voting to economics to education. We've got to challenge the education system because we need to ensure that we prepare an eighteen-year-old today for the world he or she is going to inherit in their forties. Personally, I have to think about what am I doing between now and that point in the future to put my nieces and nephews in a position to take advantage of the changing demographics in America.

Black people have always been optimistic, always believing there will be a better tomorrow. But we have to turbocharge what we're doing right now. We have to be even more aggressive in fighting things today so that future generations don't have to fight the same battles.

Every action we take today has to be driven by legacy and lineage. In your mind, your actions have to be based on tomorrow, on the year 2043. Black Americans can no longer look at the world through a selfish lens. We have to be focused on repositioning our wealth, power, and influence to put things in perspective for the next generation.

A Black teacher who is interested in becoming a principal should now be challenged to think about becoming a superintendent or creating a company that contracts with the local school system. We have to be planning ten steps ahead to create thirty more motivated and enthusiastic educators. Our sights have to be much larger, and everything has to be accelerated.

If you're a young Black man or a young Black woman in America, you can look back on the extraordinary progress, institutional progress, that Black Americans have made in this country over the past fifty years. Then you can turn on the TV and see that Black Americans aren't safe walking down the street at times. They aren't even safe going into churches. Or back to their own homes. And White Americans (especially liberals) have to stop with this ridiculous notion of a post-racial America, this whole idea that it's all kumbaya, and come to understand that in the hearts and minds of some people, you still have hatred.

For the Black community reading this book, I feel a lot of us get exhausted from being the ones in the streets. We get exhausted being the ones to pick up the community, making sure that they get to the voting booth. How do we keep strong? How do we keep our hope alive? Because we know these race wars are going to continue.

So, for Black people, it's business as usual. This is what we do. Our job is to stay the course, but more importantly our job is to be even more aggressive. Our job is to be even more unyielding. Our job is to be even more adamant about where we stand. We have absolutely no choice, none whatsoever, to stay where we are.

THE NEXT AGENDA FOR WHITE AMERICA

White Fear isn't just revealed through the talking heads on conservative cable networks. The silence and indifference of liberal

White America is just as destructive as any gun-slinging, Confederate flag-waving conservative. While the economic or societal implications of a more diverse America may not pose an immediate threat to the average White liberal, the force of White Fear will certainly rear its head when their liberal agenda feels challenged.

We, as a country, are changing. And I'm not entirely sure people get what this means. It's easy to sit here and look at today's voter suppression issues, the language and the rancor around illegal immigration, and so on, and on, and on, and think, *Things have to change.* I want this book to be the rallying cry of "Change is now, and we are change."

Outside of legislation, what are the other things that we need to do to prevent another Charlottesville or another Emanuel AME massacre? This moment requires White people of conscience to have the guts to stand up to it and stop turning a blind eye to the racism and the bigotry, and then defeat this hate at the ballot box. We're living in what is now a moment of extreme clarity for White America. White America today cannot do what White America has always done, which is to look away and say, "Not in my backyard, but I'm all good with it." White Americans today have to make the decision that they are not going to reward bigotry. They're not going to reward racism. And the fact that Donald Trump got 53 percent of White female votes in 2016, then got 55 percent in 2020, seems to be the rewarding of racism. Basically, there is no penalty for being a bigot. So the challenge for White America is, "What y'all going to do?"

America needs to confront all those companies that released their statements after George Floyd's murder. Many claimed to be committed to the Black Lives Matter movement, but do Black employees matter? Do Black board members matter? Do Black senior executives matter? Do Black businesses matter? Let's go under the hood and look at their companies' makeup, their executives' makeup, and their minority supplier development. Let's look at what they actually do.

A twelve- or fifteen-year-old White person when Obama was elected is now in their late twenties. Having an African American president during their teenage years undoubtedly had an impact; these White Americans are now saying, "We have to step up where our parents didn't to confront the systemic racism happening in America."

But what we need is for White folks to now do the heavy lifting. We need White folks to take the lead on calling out racism and bigotry. The reason the George Floyd protests resonated the way they did was because they were not actually Black dominated. What we need is for White people to stop thinking it's going to somehow be fixed in a couple of months or even a couple of years by someone else. You've got to be as invested in this as Black people have been for it to change. The true challenge is for White America to get a massive mirror, look at themselves, and ask, "Am I going to revel in my Whiteness and remain silent or ambivalent or am I going to truly try to make a change?" White people have to establish a zero tolerance for racism and bigotry and realize that it may not even look like Charlottesville. It's not going to look like tiki torches. It's not going to look like crosses burning. It is going to be the soft bigotry found in mundane, day-to-day instances.

And young White America can't just call out grandma and grandpa. They got to call out their cousins. They got to call out their nieces. They got to call out their coworkers. They got to call out the bosses. They got to call out the politicians and leaders that they're voting for. The same level of White resistance to Black inclusion has to operate now in the reverse. So, the people who really are on the clock is White America.

White folks have serious homework to do. And they've got to deliver. We have done the heavy lifting for centuries. We need modern-day White abolitionists. We need modern-day John Browns. If you're a White person living in suburban America and you don't see a lot of Black people in your neighborhood and your kids don't have to play soccer or play a clarinet with a Black kid, what are you supposed to do? What are these White people supposed to do if they're not in contact with Black people on a daily basis?

Recognize that this is part of the problem. You have to remove yourself from your Whiteness and acknowledge that your Whiteness is real. You've got to acknowledge that your Whiteness exists—and then make an effort to reach beyond your Whiteness. We're doing ourselves and future generations a disservice if we only associate with the same kind of people that we've always known and don't venture outside of our comfort zone to eat with other people, worship with other people, or understand where other people are coming from. We are living a lie every day if we don't acknowledge the truth of how we're living in this country.

ABOUT THE AUTHOR

Photo by Lanisha Cole

Roland S. Martin is the award-winning host and managing editor of *#RolandMartinUnfiltered*, the first daily online show in history focused on news and analysis of politics, entertainment, sports, and culture from an African American perspective. He is also the CEO of Black Star Network, an OTT platform. Martin provides daily radio commentaries on iHeartRadio's Black Information Network, available in 32 markets. A former CNN contributor, he continues to provide analysis on numerous national and international media outlets, including ABC News, MSNBC, BBC, and others. He is the author of *Listening to the Spirit Within: 50 Perspectives on Faith, Speak, Brother!: A Black Man's View of America*, and *The First: President Barack Obama's Road to the White House as Originally Reported by Roland S. Martin*. He is a member of the Texas A&M University Journalism Ring Of Honor; a 2021 inductee into the National Association of Black Journalists Hall of Fame; and was named a 2022 Fellow of the Society of Professional Journalists, their highest honor.